ASHES
frontline

ASHES *frontline*

The Ashes Diaries of
Justin Langer & Steve Harmison

Devised and Narrated by
Malcolm Spencer

Green**Umbrella**
Publishing

Contents

www.squareleg.com

Devised and Narrated by: Malcolm Spencer

Steve Harmison interviews conducted and compiled by: Richard Latham, Bristol and West News Agency Ltd

With special thanks to:

Cheri Gardiner – CHERI GARDINER & ASSOCIATES PTY.LTD.
Neil Fairbrother – International Sports Management
Richard Gould – Chief Executive, Somerset CCC
Chris Gelardi, Malcolm & Jane Moore

Images in this book provided courtesy of: Getty Images, 101 Bayham Street, London NW1 0AG

Creative and Art Direction: Kevin Gardner

Picture Research: Ellie Charleston

This edition first published in the UK and Australia in 2007 By Green Umbrella Publishing

© Green Umbrella Publishing 2007

www.greenumbrella.co.uk

Publishers: Jules Gammond and Vanessa Gardner

Printed and bound in China

ISBN 978-1-905828-53-1

Contents

Brisbane

Adelaide

Perth

Melbourne

Sydney

Pre-Series
Introduction

Sydney

Melbourne

Perth

Adelaide

Brisbane

Steve Harmison

Saturday

18 November 2006

Two days to go to the start of another Ashes Series and I feel fit and confident of another huge England effort to retain that precious little urn. All being well over the next 48 hours, I hope to bowl one of the opening overs of the Australian innings to Justin Langer or Matthew Hayden on Thursday morning and the thought uppermost in my mind will be 'Let's get up and at em!'

The tone of the last Ashes battle was set on the opening morning of the First Test at Lord's and we intend that to be the case again whether we are batting or bowling. Although they went on to win that match, they knew they were in for one hell of a battle. I remember the England players being amazed at the antics of the elderly Lord's members, who are normally asleep as you walk out and moaning as you walk back. Suddenly, they were patting us on the back, giving us standing ovations and even taking part in the odd Mexican wave! The fans were up for it as much as the players.

We aim to be just as aggressive and in the faces of our opponents from the start this time around. A quick wicket would be great and if we get it you can be sure there will be a few chirpy comments from the lads aimed at keeping Australia on the back foot and making them aware that there are eleven Englishmen out there up and ready for this fight.

While a drawn series would see us keep the Ashes, we have come to Australia to win. If we think about settling for a 1-1 or 2-2 finish we could well come unstuck. When the First Test starts we must push to one side the fact that we are the holders of the urn and set out to win over five huge matches. If we do that and it ends up a drawn series then so be it and we will be very happy. But, going into the series, our attitude is that whatever it takes to retain the Ashes we are ready to do it.

To me, winning the Ashes, or in this case retaining them, is the ultimate cricketing achievement for an Englishman. I would put it way ahead of winning a World Cup

HAPPY DAYS: Harmison and Flintoff relax and celebrate after the Oval Test in 2005

READY TO DO BATTLE FOR HIS COUNTRY:
Langer demonstrates his allegiance

because to do that you need only win three or four difficult one-day games, perhaps with a measure of luck along the way. With the Ashes you are talking about six or seven weeks of hard cricket where you need to give everything to be on top in every day's play.

If we can start this series well we have so much energy, youth and vibrancy in the squad that hopefully it will see us home should things become tough in the closing stages. We have prepared well and played progressively better as the warm-up games have progressed. The first match against the Prime Minister's XI was a bit of a cock-up, but we had only had time for two nets before that and we didn't know what day it was still as we became acclimatised. We enjoyed Sydney and the game against New South Wales where our cricket improved, but it was really the South Australia game in Adelaide

that provided the perfect build-up to the First Test. The whole trip there was fantastic. We had great gym facilities and the lads worked really hard in the nets. Home captain Darren Lehmann, who English cricket fans know well from his time in our county game, and coach Wayne Phillips put on a great show for us. The lads had a great time and South Australia will be very well thought of by the England camp if we do go on and win the Ashes because they gave us the perfect preparation.

My wife Hayley and daughters Emily (7), Abbie (4) and Isabel (6 months) arrived last Saturday and having them with me is a great boost. They will be here for the duration of the series and it will be a terrific education for the kids as well as wonderful for me having them around. When you get home in the evening after a long day in the field, it doesn't matter whether

you have taken five wickets or 0-100, your children love you just the same. It keeps things in perspective.

Justin Langer

Saturday
18 November 2006

Sitting on the balcony of the Oval changing room on 12 September 2005 the kindling was set somewhere deep down in my soul. With the ground awash with blue, red and white streamers, Michael Vaughan and his team drank champagne and danced around like elated school boys. And, why wouldn't they? After nineteen years they had re-secured the Ashes and reclaimed bragging rights over their longest and strongest rival, Australia.

Pre-Series Introduction

There is no doubt losing the Ashes hurt us but in the greater scheme of things I also have no doubt that Australia losing one of sport's greatest prizes was one of the best things that could have happened for international cricket and the game in general. While I would have liked to have seen a different result, I wouldn't have changed that last series for anything.

There's an old saying that 'the best thing in the world is playing and winning. The second best thing in the world is playing and losing, as long as you are still playing.' And, that is how it was the last time we met. Sure we would have preferred to win, that goes without saying, but having lost I can honestly say that I have never played in such a tightly fought contest where incredible lessons were learned on both sides of the fence.

With only a few days to go before the re-match, I can't imagine there would be as much hype for this series had we retained the title last time. With England stricken by the early loss of their captain, Michael Vaughan, and their fire-brand reverse swinger Simon Jones, there would have been a danger the series might have lost some of its polish. The sudden and deeply disappointing departure of Marcus Trescothick could have heightened the dread of another easy Ashes hold for Australia had we still held the trophy.

These would-have and could-have scenarios are no longer applicable now because the fact is that no matter how anyone looks at the series Australia have to win the extended battle to re-hold the urn. Ashes contests are always eagerly awaited but in essence it was England's gallant fight last August and September that has allowed cricket to dominate the back pages of the press for the last month or so.

From a personal view, that kindling, set on 12 September, is burning stronger than ever and now the contest is upon us, the atmosphere within the Australian camp is one of real excitement. We have our backs to the wall in the sense that we have to wrestle the urn back and we know the Australian public wants to see the Ashes bragging rights come back home within the next six weeks.

Although there has been so much hype leading into the first Test at the Gabba on Thursday, I know all the words in the world will count for little when Steve Harmison or Glenn McGrath deliver that first ball of the series. Hopefully I will be the one taking that first ball on Thursday morning. There can be few greater thrills for me than facing the first ball of such a massive Test contest. At Lord's 15 months ago that first delivery rocketed into the gloves of Geraint Jones and it was at that point that I knew England really meant business. If their body language is anything like it was on that morning then we will know we are in for a really tough contest again.

In a couple of hours I will walk off this flight from Perth knowing that our final Ashes preparations are now only one sleep away and like a little kid at Christmas I simply can't wait. For the next five days we will train hard and add the sparkle to a preparation that started taking shape the day after we lost the Ashes in London. We have spent our time soul-searching and analysing where we went wrong and we feel

PLENTY TO THINK ABOUT: Harmison works with Kevin Shine in the nets before the Brisbane Test

after winning 12 of the last 13 Test matches that we can't be more ready for this encounter. The tingles in the back of my neck are making their way down to my feet as the fire within reminds me of just how important this series is to me and my team-mates.

Steve Harmison

Sunday

19 November 2006

Obviously, my preparation for the series has not been trouble-free because I had to miss the South Australia game. I had a problem with my side during the summer in

England, but then had five or six weeks off before going to India and was fine over there. For some reason it flared up again when we got here and halfway through the second day of the New South Wales game it started to hurt. It gradually got worse and after we moved to Adelaide I had more discomfort in the nets the day before the South Australia match. Instead of playing, I had an injection, bowled 20 overs in the nets the following day and 15 more the day after that. Now I have had 40 minutes in the nets this morning and, although there is still a bit of stiffness, I feel fine. All I have missed really is two days in the field and that may even be a good thing because I feel fresh going into the First Test.

Losing Michael Vaughan and Simon Jones from our Ashes winning squad is a major blow, but one we have been preparing for over the last six months. Not so the departure of Marcus Trescothick, who has been a huge player for us, and one we would have loved to have in the front line this time around. That has been difficult to take, although none of the players has anything but immense sympathy for Marcus. There is absolutely no doubt about his cricketing ability and the most important thing now is for him to sort himself out as a person. The lads could see he was a bit down from the start of the tour and, having suffered with homesickness myself on past trips, I probably was better placed to have a word with him than most. Some people say it was a gamble selecting him, but I don't see it that way. His record is such that he had to be picked if he felt ready. No one in the England camp blames him and our only thought is for him to get through this and return to where he belongs, on the pitch with us. My

problems didn't get anywhere near as severe as Marcus's, but they were bad enough for me to say I would prefer to have been injured than suffering in the way I did. You can't tell people what is wrong with something like depression. Only those who have experienced it know and there were a couple of times when Marcus and I had a quiet chat because he knew I understood. I felt so sorry for him when he left, but he is in the best place possible with his family around him and I am sure he will be watching the series on the box and rooting for us.

Justin Langer

Monday

20 November 2006

Playing with the Australian cricket team invokes many privileges and one of those is the resources available at every training session. Today we trained for the first time as a Test squad in nearly six months and the intensity of the session was superb. Rather than practicing at the Gabba we used the facilities at Brisbane Grammar school. The advantage of this was two centre wickets and a myriad of turf and synthetic practice nets.

With many invited net bowlers of varying ages and abilities, every batsman was basically able to bat for as long or as short a time as they liked. For someone like me who likes to hit a lot of balls leading into a Test match today was like cricket heaven. All up I must have batted for an hour and a half in the middle and in the nets, a luxury rarely available to any cricketer around the world. This type of preparation means no stone

Pre-Series Introduction

LAST MINUTE CHECKS: Langer continues his preparation in the nets with John Buchanan

has been left unturned leading into the game.

Practice was followed by a long media session where every player is grilled about everything to do with the Ashes. I was a little taken back in my first interview of the day by a female reporter from SBS. She was like the smiling assassin, hounding me about the pressure I was under for my place in the team. She spoke of nothing but the form of Phil Jacques; I can only guess she is related to him or perhaps a good die-hard New South Wales supporter.

Leading into this series there has been a great deal of speculation about my place in the team. There is no doubt Phil Jacques has been in fantastic form but at the end of the day so have I and my opening partnership with Matty Hayden has been a successful one for a long period of time. I was confident I had the support of Ricky and the team in terms of remaining at the top of the order but it was still nice to see my name on paper when the team was selected a few days ago. Now I can just get on with batting and dispel all of the speculation by making plenty of runs in the first Test.

In some ways I am thankful for the constant speculation over my position. I have endured it throughout my career and I am sure the added pressure has helped me become a mentally tough player. It is impossible to survive as an international cricketer unless you have a high degree of mental toughness and from this point of view I am glad I have had to fight so hard for so long.

Having said all that it is still frustrating to hear these whispers so regularly. I am sure the people who throw out these suggestions don't really have a close look at the job I have done for the team over a long period of time. I know it is none of my business what other people think of me but sometimes it definitely wears you down.

In our first pre-Ashes team meeting one of Ricky's themes was that this series gave us an opportunity to silence some of our critics. No silence will last forever but it may quieten the many detractors out there who continually question the team. 'Lets see if they are still putting us down at the end of the series' was the sentiment shared to us by the skipper who looks to be very focused and committed to the next five Test matches.

Steve Harmison

Tuesday
21 November 2006

The players who have come in as a result of injuries are very talented in their own right. For example, Jimmy Anderson, who has replaced Simon Jones, can swing the ball both ways and get reverse swing. Alastair Cook, Ian Bell and Paul Collingwood are all in great nick so, as much as you always want to field your strongest side, injuries are part of sport and everything looks to me as though it is on the up and up.

Having Freddie Flintoff fit is a massive boost because being without him alters the whole balance of the team. He is also an inspirational leader who can lift the side sometimes with just a look or some of the stupid things he does in the dressing room. He makes good players around him better and I would go as far as to say that the coming series revolves around him. When something needs to happen, nine times out of ten he will put his hand up and try to do it himself. He leads from the front more than

FEELING FIT: Harmison tests out his side strain, following his absence from the Adelaide warm-up game

Brisbane

Adelaide

Perth

Melbourne

Sydney

Michael Vaughan, who has an uncanny knack of getting the best out of people without you quite knowing why. Michael's success as skipper stemmed from understanding how to treat each individual in the right way to maximise his contribution. Freddie just never asks anyone to do what he wouldn't do himself. Very different characters, but both tremendously inspirational captains.

The Australian crowds have so far been largely humorous and full of the normal banter. In the streets the England players have been very courteously received and they wish us well, without wanting it to be too well. The England players know we are going to cop it when we field on the edge and there is nothing wrong with a few remarks from the crowd as long as they are within reason. We even enjoy it. They are very partisan and patriotic towards their own team and England players are ready to take a ribbing. But we expect our own supporters to be out in number and we know they will have a few things to say to the Aussie players too.

The Australian team we will be facing is vastly experienced and much has been made about a number of the players becoming quite old for Test cricket. In the England camp we view them simply as very good cricketers, but we also know that if we can put pressure on them, and keep it on, that age factor may play a part in the later stages of the series. There is no hiding the fact that several of them are over 30 and, if we can limit their performances in the first couple of Tests, outside influences such as the media will come into play. That's another reason why we need to get the upper hand early on. If we do, the age issue will become a bigger thing and the

presence of certain players in their team may well be questioned.

One thing Australia have done so well for 10 or 12 years is kick opposing teams when they are down. That's why they have enjoyed such success and it's a mentality we need to match. We have to get them down and then kick them hard in the weeks ahead.

Justin Langer
Wednesday
22 November 2006

One of the things I love the most about playing Test cricket is the lead up to a Test series. Rarely is

the build-up as grand as it has been for this series, but in essence the preparations are always similar.

For the last three days we have hit cricket balls, taken hundreds of catches and the bowlers have worked hard on gaining that all important rhythm they all strive so hard to achieve. We have spent time on the massage bench, soaked in ice baths and stretched and pampered our bodies so that we feel fresh and ready for the contest in the morning.

At around eleven o'clock this morning, when all of the physical preparations had been completed, I took my final personal journey out into the middle of the Gabba. Walking barefooted with my Ipod blaring in my ears, I held my favourite bat and a new pair of batting gloves and I danced around

WHAT IS OUT THERE?: Justin Langer ponders on what the next few weeks will bring

on the pitch and visualized everything I thought I could expect when the action kicks off in the morning. I have learned this technique from Matty Hayden who swears by this mental routine before every game.

Imagine the opportunity of this: walking into the centre of the world's great cricket grounds, the day before a big Test match, with your bare feet touching the hallowed turf and no one ever daring to question your motives or moves.

Like so many things these concessions are nothing but a privilege for a Test cricketer and it is one of the things I will miss when my days in this game are over.

The tension is certainly building, but from our camp I know we are ready. Our preparation has been intense and sharp and we are ready to go. I simply cannot wait to face the first ball of the series and regardless of the result I know I will be alive when I walk out to the roar of the crowd at the Gabba, which is looking an absolute treat.

I also know that in spite of our fantastic preparation, I will have to set my alarm earlier in the morning than usual so that I can keep tapping the snooze button to allow me extra time in my bed. It fascinates me how the human mind has such a bearing on how we feel physically. In the morning experience tells me I won't want to get out of bed, I will visit the toilet four or five times and I won't be able to drink coffee or eat much breakfast. It's amazing how the mind works but in the same breath I wouldn't change tomorrow's opportunity for anything.

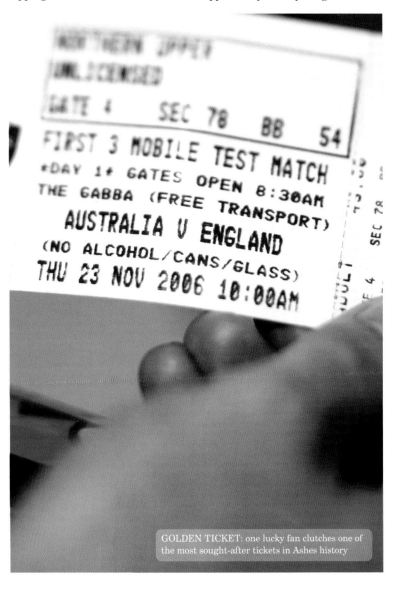

GOLDEN TICKET: one lucky fan clutches one of the most sought-after tickets in Ashes history

FIRST TEST
Brisbane
The Gabba

View from the Boundary

Teams

Umpires: B F Bowden, S A Bucknor

Australia: M L Hayden, J L Langer, R T Ponting, D R Martyn, M E K Hussey, M J Clarke, A C Gilchrist, S K Warne, B Lee, S R Clark, G D McGrath

England: A J Strauss, A N Cook, I R Bell, P D Collingwood, K P Pietersen, A Flintoff, G O Jones, A F Giles, M J Hoggard, S J Harmison, J M Anderson

Australia won the toss and elected to bat

Thursday

23 November 2006

FIRST TEST, DAY ONE

Following 14 months of continuous speculation and build-up to this series, Ponting wasted no time in electing to bat on this very flat and dry pitch. History would suggest that the team that survives the first hour on this surface should go on to amass a large first-innings total on what has, in recent years, become Australia's best batting wicket.

With the weather a hot and sunny 29 degrees and a forecast for more of the same for the duration of this match, a good start could mean the beginning of a long fielding session for England.

After bowling the first delivery of the match to 2nd slip, Harmison and England's other premier fast bowlers Hoggard and Anderson, through a mixture of nerves and ill discipline, struggled with their line and length and, with an un-characteristically low level of humidity for Brisbane, got almost no movement in the air or off the seam.

With the opening bowlers letting Australia off to a flyer, they allowed Justin Langer and Matthew Hayden to score at nearly 5 an over.

Finally Flintoff restored some level of control and threat in the attack, quickly taking the wicket of Hayden, caught comfortably at second slip by Collingwood,

standing in that position after the reshuffle of the slips cordon following Trescothick's departure.

Langer, outscoring his partner 2-1, after an initial selection of moderately streaky shots, began to look comfortable on this true and reliable surface and, by the interval, had compiled a confident 68 not out.

England improved their bowling considerably in the second session of this match, bringing the run rate down from nearly 5 to just over 4 an over.

Flintoff continued to bowl well and, against the indication of Justin's form, took the wicket of Langer for 82 who, in attempting to drive Freddie off the back foot

NOT IN GOOD SHAPE: Umpires Billy Bowden and Steve Bucknor inspect the ball

through the covers, got a little underneath the delivery and presented a firm but comfortable catch to Kevin Pietersen at Cover point.

Harmison returned for a further spell and bowled with considerably more control and, on occasions, a little more pace.

Looking for a little variety as the ball began to lose its hardness, Flintoff brought Giles into the attack after the drinks break. With an action modified by a combination of recent hip operations and the threat of his place to Monty Panesar, he bowled with aggression and picked up the wicket of Damien Martyn fairly early into his spell, late cutting into the hands of an alert Collingwood at slip for 29.

The wicket offered almost no turn whatsoever on a surface that was more of a 'day 2' style but, as is typical of the Gabba pitch, there was plenty in the way of bounce for the slower bowlers.

Ponting, who looked confident from the moment he arrived at the crease, progressed fluently to his first fifty of the series and, with Hussey, took the Australians past two hundred as they went into tea.

This session was dominated by the Australians.

Flintoff, opting to bowl himself in short 3-4 over spells, used seven bowlers in an effort to prise out a wicket on this belter of a Brisbane surface. However, with his frontline bowlers proving to be lacking in discipline on this first day, a fourth wicket proved elusive.

Ponting, who began this game under a considerable amount of pressure from the media and other cricket observers, delivered the perfect reminder to the Australian public and reporters alike as to why he is their country's most successful number 3. With superb

LEADING FROM THE FRONT: Freddie celebrates the wicket of Hayden

timing and shots all around this magnificent ground, he went on to complete a fine century and finish the day unbeaten on 137.

Hussey, very much playing the supporting role for his captain also notched up a well-constructed and conservatively-built 63.

Australia finished the day very much in control and left England the very likely prospect of another long, hot day in the field.

Brisbane

Adelaide

Perth

Melbourne

Sydney

Steve Harmison

Thursday
23 November 2006

FIRST TEST, DAY ONE

This was it. What I've been working towards for 14 months. I felt excited, as well as a bit nervous, but firmly in my mind was to do what we did in the last Ashes series and set the tone on the opening morning. We did the warm-ups and I felt ready. Standing out there with the England team while the national anthems were played I just felt an immense sense of pride at representing my country. Here I was in Australia about to play in an Ashes Series. The feeling was unbelievable. Not a spare seat to be seen among a 40,000 crowd and the scene set for another memorable contest. Thinking back now, if I'm honest, I believe I got caught up in the emotion of the occasion and it stopped me focussing properly on the job in hand.

When Freddie threw me the ball and told me I was bowling the first delivery of the series I still felt confident. I felt well prepared and ready to do my best. Unfortunately, it didn't work out that way and

ONE TO FORGET: Steve sees his first delivery of the series aim towards the hands of his good mate Freddie at second slip

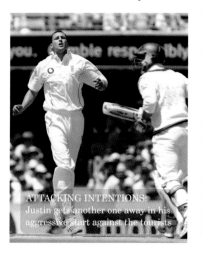

ATTACKING INTENTIONS: Justin gets another one away in his aggressive start against the tourists

the match as a whole would go down as my worst experience on a cricket field.

My hands were sweaty and I couldn't grip the ball properly as I prepared to bowl to Justin Langer. Suddenly, I just had a mental block and froze a bit just when it mattered most. That first ball ended up in Freddie's hands at second slip and, as it turned out, there was no way back for me. The same thing happened with the second delivery, which fortunately went a bit straighter, but, by then, I was shaking a bit and very nervous so I became apprehensive about letting the ball go.

My first two overs I went for 4 fours, but they were mainly through third-man off half-decent deliveries. I was disappointed Freddie took me off at that stage because I felt I could have got

better given a longer spell, and the last thing I wanted was an hour until my next bowl to reflect on those two overs. I found myself fielding down on the boundary with the crowd letting loose all sorts of comments. Hundreds of things were going through my mind and I have to admit that, having been caught up in the occasion, I forgot what I was out there to do. I was thinking of what had gone wrong, what to do to bring it back, trying to stay calm, trying to get enough fluid in my body because it was a very hot day, so many things all at once. It was like my worst nightmare coming true and even now, soon after the event, it's all a bit of a blur.

Australia ended the day on 346-3. As good as they were, we didn't bowl well as a team and I didn't turn up on the day.

significant. His first seed flew wide and into the safe hands of his captain Andrew Flintoff at second slip, while the second flew wildly down the leg-side at a less than rapid pace. Although the atmosphere was electric I could sense even then that England don't look as confident and intense about this contest as the last time we met.

Of course I may be way off the mark, but after today's fantastic day for Australia it is great to have taken early momentum in this series. Ricky Ponting is simply a freak with a cricket bat in his hand. His genius today was best defined by his two on drives early in his innings. The first was eased back past the bowler, the second hammered wide of mid-on. Considering the on drive is the

hardest shot to play in the game of cricket, I knew our captain was in for a special day. He is undoubtedly the master batsman of the modern era, along with Sachin and B C Lara.

Today was a special day. Queensland, like all of Australia, has gone Ashes mad and the atmosphere is unbelievable. One of the most special memories of today was the national anthem ceremony. Never before have I heard the crowd drown out the special guest singer, but today the entire Gabba was alight with our wonderful anthem. Standing shoulder to shoulder with my team-mates belting out the anthem in our strongest voices was a perfect start to what really has been a perfect day for the home team.

Thursday
23 November 2006

FIRST TEST, DAY ONE

For the last 14 months I have been talking about the last Ashes series and in particular how significant the first ball of the contest was. Back then Steve Harmison roared in and bowled a thunderbolt which smashed into the gloves of Geraint Jones. The second ball was equally as fierce except that it rocketed into my right elbow rather than his wicket-keeper's gloves. From those two balls alone, England's body language was lethal and we knew they meant business.

After today I can't help but wonder if "Harmy"'s first two balls won't ultimately prove as

WELCOME RELIEF: Flintoff celebrates the first wicket of the tour

Friday
24 November 2006

FIRST TEST, DAY TWO

Resuming on 363-3 England were conscious that they had to produce a considerably improved bowling performance if they were to avoid spending the day in the field.

Ponting picking up from his 137 overnight immediately looked to return to the groove that had helped him pile on the runs so effortlessly the previous day and, before long, had moved onto 150.

With a little more humidity in the air both Hoggard and Anderson began to get some swing from this second new ball. However, with both Australians playing watchfully in the opening overs, Ponting and Hussey saw themselves through to the drinks break without incident.

Flintoff, by far and away the best bowler in the match so far, brought himself into the attack following the break and immediately extracted a little more life from this drying surface. Bowling a good line and hitting the widening cracks in the Gabba wicket both batsmen were hurried into the occasional shot.

Finally, Flintoff produced a peach of a delivery that seamed back into the left-handed Hussey just enough to find a gap through his defences and remove his off stump for a patient and well crafted 86.

Lifted by the wicket, Flintoff continued to apply pressure to the batsmen, beating the new man Clarke on his first delivery and troubling the well-set Ponting.

Clarke, in the side for the injured Watson, looked keen not to waste his opportunity and, applying great concentration and a purposeful approach joined Ponting in reaching the lunch break unscathed.

Following lunch Ricky Ponting resumed his almost faultless display of stroke-making against the English in his pursuit of his first double-hundred against the countrymen. Playing shots to all parts of the ground, none of the English bowlers appeared to have an answer to his run making.

However, late on into the first hour after lunch, with the ball still offering some assistance to those bowlers who could control the seam, Matthew Hoggard, in the middle of a tight and threatening spell, produced an excellent over to dismiss both Ponting and the hugely imposing Adam Gilchrist. Ponting, who had progressed to the 190s just walked across his stumps a little to a ball that swung back in to him a fraction and, with a look of despair, was adjudged lbw for a magnificent 196. Adam Gilchrist, whose very presence at the crease heightens the anticipation of the crowd, swung and missed at his third delivery to a ball that ducked in towards his pads and he too was making his way back for no score.

Shane Warne, in typically entertaining style, looked to get on top of the bowling straight away and, with the comfort of a big

A LITTLE EXTRA:
Umpire Bucknor signals a wide

total behind him, played with freedom and his own brand of flamboyance. Lucky not to have been caught on a couple of occasions he finally succumbed to a much improved and hostile spell from Steve Harmison, gloving an attempted hook shot to Jones behind the stumps for 17.

Clarke, who had looked to be more positive following the departure of his senior colleagues, continued to fifty, now partnered by the ever reliable Brett Lee at the other end.

Passing 500, and with perhaps the thought of a declaration in the back of their minds, both players played with a little more aggression as they approached the tea interval when, finally, in the last over before the break, Clarke, looking to drive James Anderson through the covers, was deceived by the bowler's consistent late swing and edged a comfortable chance to Strauss at first slip for a well made 56.

After tea, Clark, playing in his debut Test match, performed the most wonderful little cameo for his country, striking an impressive 39 from just 23 deliveries before finally being bowled by a Yorker from Flintoff.

Brett Lee, who has often proved to be a difficult man to dislodge down the order, was now joined by the ever optimistic batsman Glen McGrath. Lee, with a combination of orthodox stroke play and some fortunate ricochets, made his way to a very competent 43 before, on the passing of the psychologically import 600 run mark, Ponting called his men in to get ready to attack with the ball.

With a tricky short spell of bowling to face before the close of play, England openers Andrew Strauss and Alistair Cook got off to a confident start. Brett Lee, the fastest of the bowlers in both teams bowled at tight line at around 150kph but it was the veteran Glen McGrath who struck first with the important wicket of Strauss. Attempting a pull shot from a ball outside the off stump, Strauss got underneath it and sent up a skyer to square leg. Hussey, running around from mid-wicket, and Brett Lee coming up from fine leg briefly tangled as Hussey, first to the ball, managed to hang on to a good running catch to send Strauss back to the pavilion for just 12.

With his very next ball, having changed his line to around the wicket, McGrath managed to get a ball to angle away from the left-hander and Cook, forced to play at it, edged a sharp catch to Warne at first slip for 11.

England, chasing a mammoth 402 to avoid the follow on, were now 28-2.

Clark, brought on to replace Lee who had cut his leg in his collision with Hussey, now claimed the slot for his own by bowling an extremely tight line with a little movement off the seam. Soon, his disciplined effort, which had brought about a collection of swings and misses, got the edge he was looking for as Collingwood pushed down the line to a full length delivery that moved slightly away off the seam and sent a regulation catch through to Gilchrist.

England, now 42-3 and in deep trouble, had Bell and Pietersen at the crease but, with just 23 minutes of the day's play remaining, both batsmen survived a testing session through to stumps.

View from the Boundary

IS THIS MY SEAT?: A Barmy Army member grins in anticipation at a day spent amongst the Aussie fans

Brisbane

Adelaide

Perth

Melbourne

Sydney

Friday

24 November 2006

FIRST TEST, DAY TWO

Ricky Ponting is quite simply the best player I have ever played against. On front and back foot he is equally aggressive as a batsman. Ponting is a top player, very good captain and tough cookie. Today he took his overnight score of 137 to 196 and showed us just what he is made of. We didn't bowl well at him, but you still have to put bad balls away and he did that without mercy.

The fourth wicket stand with Mike Hussey took Australia from 198-3 on the first day to 407 and piled things up against us. I've played with Hussey at Durham and he deserves the nickname 'Mr Cricket'. All he wants to do when not playing is practice and show his enthusiasm for the team and, when

TEXT-BOOK STUFF: Ponting continues his commanding innings of 196

you see him coming in with three wickets down and a big score already on the board, you think 'Oh my God'.

At the start of the day our main thoughts were on trying to pick ourselves up after such a poor first day. For me, unfortunately, it was more of the same. I didn't start the day well and was badly lacking in confidence. In fact, I was rock bottom in that respect. The day just went exactly the way the Australians wanted. The one positive was that we got a big danger-man in Gilchrist out for a duck in a way we had planned. In fact, it was true to say our plans for getting out all the top Australian batsmen worked in the end. We had planned to drag Ponting across his stumps in a bid to get him lbw, he just happened to be on 196 at the time, which wasn't part of the plan!

We tried to stick to our plans and restricted the scoring rate for a bit, but as we tired their bowlers came in and swung the bat. Stuart Clark had a swing and it came off. You can just as easily hit one up in the air and be caught for nothing, but it was Clark's day. We were out of synch as a team and when that happens as individuals you have to look to get the best out of a day. Freddie did that with his figures of 4-99. He bowled well, Hoggy came back impressively and Jimmy's figures were very harsh on him. I

FEELING THE HEAT: Steve gathers his thoughts between deliveries

just didn't perform again, but the others got the best out of another bad day.

We ended on 53-3 in reply to 602 so it was a pretty dire position. When you've been on the receiving end in the field for a day and three quarters the last thing you want is to have to bat for an hour and face Brett Lee with a brand new ball in his hand. The pitch was absolutely made for someone with the accuracy of Glenn McGrath, who could find the cracks and exploit them. The 'Dad's Army' tag given to the Australian team before the match had wound him up and he was facing some tired bodies and minds. We weren't happy with 53-3, but it is very hard when the Aussies are on a roll like they were when our innings started.

Brisbane

Adelaide

Perth

Melbourne

Sydney

champion. He was ruthless again and set the scene for another outstanding day for the home team.

Michael Hussey continued his awesome form at Test level with a beautifully constructed 86 and Michael Clarke made the most of his opportunity with a timely half century. To rub salt into England's wounds, our tail hung around allowing us to reach the monumental first innings total of 600; a target which may seem like the summit of Mount Everest for England.

When it came to our turn to bowl, our pace trio caused plenty of headaches for England's top order and at stumps they have lost three of their top order. We feel on top at the moment but understand there is still plenty of cricket to be played in this Test. So far everything has gone to plan but we have to keep up our intensity to drown England out of this game.

Friday
24 November 2006

FIRST TEST, DAY TWO

Ricky Ponting may have fallen short of his double century by four runs, but once again he has cemented his reputation as one of Australia's greatest ever batsman. His innings over the last two days not only showed immense skill and a steely concentration, but also reflected the attitude within the Australian team.

After batting for nearly five hours yesterday, our captain padded up again this morning and batted with a resolve reserved for a

GRABBING HIS OPPORTUNITY: Clarke turns one onto the leg side on his way to 56

View from the Boundary

Sydney

Melbourne

Perth

Adelaide

Brisbane

COUNTER-ATTACK: Pietersen looks to get England back into the game

Saturday
25 November 2006

FIRST TEST, DAY THREE

With nearly 350 runs required just to avoid the follow on, it was crucial that England got off to a good start in the morning. Pietersen and Bell were facing the duo of McGrath and Lee on a pitch that, following 3 days of continual sunshine, had begun to develop large cracks.

Unlike any of the previous days, this morning the ball deviated wickedly off the seam as it hit the cracks and with both Lee and McGrath bowling with great accuracy the England batsmen were focused in their attempt to see off the first hour and, with it, the hardness of the ball.

Forty-five minutes into the day however, Pietersen shouldered arms to a ball that hit one of those cracks and was adjudged lbw playing no shot for 16. One of the danger men for Australia was gone and it brought the other to the crease. Flintoff, looking understandably nervous given his team's position, played tentatively and, just a few balls later pushed out to a full pitch delivery and was caught behind off Lee without scoring.

England now 79-5 were facing the prospect of a dismal first-innings total but Bell, playing with great resolve and concentration, and Geraint Jones, knuckled down to take the score onto 118 and reach the lunch interval.

A session completely dominated by Australia.

England, resuming after the break began well enough with continued focus against an unrelentingly accurate attack from McGrath and Clark but, after just 50 minutes, Jones was caught on the back foot for 19 to a full-pitched delivery that kept just a fraction low. Mixing up his length very occasionally, McGrath had kept Jones on the back foot for most of the session and therefore was late coming forward to a ball that would have gone on to hit middle stump.

That brought Giles to the crease to play his first innings for nearly a

View from the Boundary

year. With continued pressure from both bowlers, it was Bell, who had looked confident and focused on his way to a third 50 against Australia who, perhaps drawn in by a more driveable length delivery, didn't quite get to the pitch of it and steered a sharp catch to Ponting at second slip for a half century.

That somewhat opened the flood gates and it wasn't long before the new batsman Hoggard was playing down the wrong line to Clark and edged another catch to the wicket-keeper for 0.

McGrath, who had now bowled a fairly lengthy spell since lunch, was kept on and quickly dismissed Harmison without scoring to grab his 10th 5-wicket haul against the tourists.

At nine down, Giles now looked to push the scoring on at any opportunity but, after a couple of

OUT-THOUGHT: McGrath traps Jones lbw for 19

useful shots, he attempted to make room for himself from a good

WELCOME BACK: After nine months out Giles is greeted at the crease with another hostile delivery

length delivery from McGrath and, in hoping to cut one through the off side, managed only to get under it and offer a simple skyer to Hayden at backward point for 24.

Australia, in an effort to give their pace bowlers a rest, decided not to force the follow-on. Instead Ponting gave his openers an opportunity to add a few more runs to this already massive lead.

England, opening with Hoggard and Anderson, bowled with more consistency and a better line early on but both openers continued to score freely, soon passing yet another 50 partnership to add to their impressive record.

Eventually, with the score on 68, Hayden fell victim to a sharp piece of fielding and was run out for 38.

After that the day meandered to a close with Langer (88) and Ponting (51) amassing a formidable lead of 626 by stumps.

Saturday
25 November 2006

FIRST TEST, DAY THREE

Things continued to go all Australia's way when we were bowled out for 157, with McGrath taking 6-50. I was one of his victims. He slipped one through me second ball, which bounced on me a bit and had me caught behind. I might have got away with it because I received a pat on the back from umpire Billy Bowden for walking, but to me it seemed like an obvious nick. Glenn didn't even look at the umpire he was that convinced and there was no point in hanging around with our innings in ruins. I saw first hand how Glenn was hitting the cracks because my first ball darted away and the second nipped back to clip the shoulder of my bat. It capped my day and to be honest I couldn't wait to get off.

There was criticism of Ponting's decision not to enforce the follow-on, but it didn't surprise us at all and I thought it was perfectly correct. Glenn had bowled 25 overs and, at the age of 37, with two and a half days left, I don't think he would have been too happy had he been asked to go out and bowl again.

Australia were in a no-lose situation when their second innings began with a lead of 400-plus. If they came out swinging and ended 50-5 they would still be in a great position. Matthew Hayden was aggressive and got himself into some nick, while Langer could see the opportunity for a big score and contained himself a bit. Ricky was seeing it like a football and just continued where he had left off in the first innings. The happy thing for me was that I ran in and got 12 overs under my belt, bowling nicely and finding some sort of rhythm, hopefully a good sign for the remainder of the series. If Ponting had enforced the follow-on I would have had to wait until Adelaide for my next ball and my confidence would have remained down. Instead I was able to draw some encouragement from finding my feet and remembering that I could bowl at this level. I kept the ball on one side of the wicket and felt a lot better.

For all that, Australia closed on 181-1 with a lead of 626. It had been a thankless task for our bowlers given the match situation and for the third successive day everything had gone the home side's way.

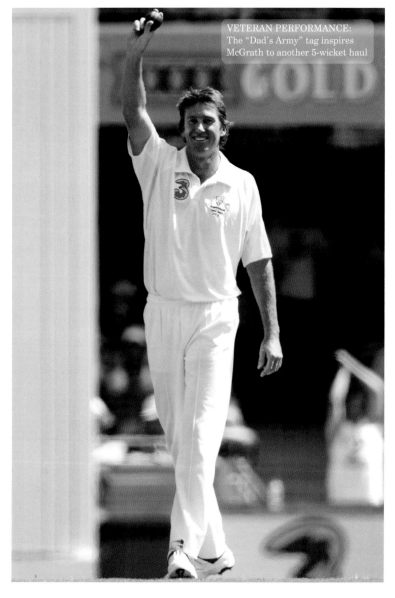

VETERAN PERFORMANCE: The "Dad's Army" tag inspires McGrath to another 5-wicket haul

Saturday
25 November 2006

FIRST TEST, DAY THREE

The accolades went to Glenn McGrath for his magnificent six-wicket haul, but I can't remember our bowlers bowling so well as a collective unit for a long time. Watching the look in Ian Bell's eyes I can only imagine he would have walked off the field understanding just how hard Test match cricket can be. He played very well for his half century, but in his time at the innings there wouldn't have been one easy run credited to his name.

For the last few months Glenn McGrath has had his detractors. Some critics have said he is too old, that he has lost his pace and that his aura has diminished. Well, if this is the case I can't help but wonder how England would have

A JOB WELL DONE: Langer and Ponting leave the field a massive 626 ahead

fared if he were actually on top of his game. He is a superstar, with a character of steel and it is one of the highlights of my career having been able to simply stand on the field with this colossus of the game.

A lot was made of the pitch at the end of today but if you look closely at the score line we have made nearly 800 runs on it for the loss of only ten wickets.

Sure there are cracks running up and down the surface but generally these are more of a psychological deterrent than anything else. As a batsman you look down the pitch and wonder what will happen if the ball 'might' hit a crack. This then has the effect of slowing the messages from your brain to your hands and feet. When this happens batting becomes a nightmare.

So far the first three days have been something of a nightmare for England. We couldn't have dreamed of a better start to this series and we will be looking to keep the foot on the accelerator until this first Test match is firmly secured in our hands.

NORMAL SERVICE RESUMED: McGrath celebrates another English victim

View from the Boundary

Sunday
26 November 2006

FIRST TEST, DAY FOUR

Australia, taking the somewhat controversial decision to continue batting into day 4, carried on much as they had left off from the previous day with Ponting allowing his team-mate the opportunity to chalk up three figures for his country. Almost immediately after the celebrations had subsided on reaching his 23rd international ton, his captain took his partner off the field to begin the bowling against England.

A massive 647 runs ahead, victory for England was a virtual impossibility but, with almost six sessions to survive, both openers rightly decided to play their natural game.

With the score on just 29, Strauss, for the second time in this match, fell to the temptation of an early pull shot and succeeded only in steering his shot to the awaiting substitute fielder at backward square leg for just 11.

Bell, who had batted so well in the first innings, lasted just 4 deliveries before, in pushing forward to a Warne delivery, he was deceived by one that went straight on, providing a simple lbw decision for the umpire.

Now 36-2 England look set to face the indignity of being beaten inside 4 days however, with some fluent stroke play from Cook and a resilient approach from Collingwood, the pair recovered England's fortunes with a smart 50 Partnership.

Cook, who had batted with great flare to reach 43, had begun to look comfortable on this still-decent batting wicket but, with players around the bat, he pushed out to a

NORTHERN GRIT: Collingwood continues with great concentration on his way to 96

good-length ball from Warne and got the slightest of inside edges onto his pads which ricocheted to the hands of Hussey at short leg.

Collingwood continued to progress well though and, on passing fifty, began to look more aggressive. Pietersen too, in his customary style also appeared determined not to allow the situation or the Australians to get on top of him and, over the next hour or so, the pair had successfully retaliated with a fabulous 100 partnership with Kevin bringing up an impressive 50.

Collingwood however was eventually to be undone by his positive approach and, agonisingly, just 4 runs short of what would have been a magnificent century in these conditions, came down the wicket to lift Warne over mid-off and was beaten by the turn, gifting Gilchrist an easy stumping opportunity.

England, now on 244-4 were joined by their captain who, in attempting to maintain the positive stance adopted by the two in the middle before him, began confidently with a selection of well-timed boundaries. He too though was to fall victim to a rush of blood and, in attempting an ambitious pull shot from a Warne short pitch delivery, was left looking with despair as it miscued off a thick leading edge to the safe hands of Justin Langer at deep mid-on.

Australia, now sensing that the back of this England innings was broken, applied further pressure to the incoming Jones but, with just 40 minutes left until the end of play, both batsmen hung on to take this Test into a final day.

DONE HIM: Warne celebrates having tempted Collingwood into a rash shot

Brisbane

Adelaide

Perth

Melbourne

Sydney

Sunday
26 November 2006

FIRST TEST, DAY FOUR

THE PERFECT RESPONSE: Langer answers his critics' calls for his place with a typically focused century before Ponting calls time on their innings

Justin Langer got the century he so badly wanted at the second attempt and fair play to him because it was a great effort. He had been under pressure going into the game. When you get to the wrong side of 33 or 34 and you get a couple of low scores your place is in jeopardy. He wanted to prove his critics wrong and did so.

With victory out of the question, we focused on keeping Australia out in the field for as long as possible in our second innings. It had been damage limitation as far as we were concerned from the first day. Now we had to show a bit of character. We were facing back-to-back Test Matches and the one thing that was stressed at the start of the innings was that the harder we made it for the Aussies the more they might feel it at Adelaide. Without making too much of the age thing, we know there are some old legs in their side and we have to test them to the full. We stressed that wickets were priceless even though the match was virtually lost and that applied right down to nine, ten, eleven.

Paul Collingwood led the way after a tough start to his innings. He came in at tea-time and I said "Well played". He looked at me with that wry smile of his and replied "Were you effing watching?" I told him he was still there and that was the main thing. Sure enough, he went back out and only just missed out on a century. I thought Shane Warne did him up like a kipper on 96 with a superb piece of bowling. Colly was devastated, but it was a great

innings ended by an equally fine bit of bowling by a player of huge talent and experience. Colly would have happily taken 96 before the start, but like Langer he is a tremendous competitor and he would have loved those extra four runs.

Kevin Pietersen finished the day 92 not out, which was another huge fillip for us. It must be a nightmare batting after KP because you must be out of your seat virtually every ball! But he is awesome to watch. As a tail-ender I just sit there watching the ball disappear to all parts and find it unbelievable.

Watching two world-class performers go head to head for a couple of hours was riveting. The feeling in the dressing room was that if he can keep playing like this we have a great chance of retaining the Ashes.

We closed on 293-5 and it could have been even better because Freddie got out to a ball he could have hit anywhere he wanted. He came off desperately disappointed because he wanted to score a big one, but he looked so good in making 16. Hopefully, Freddie is saving his runs for when we need them.

Sunday
26 November 2006

FIRST TEST, DAY FOUR

England, through the fight of Paul Collingwood and Kevin Pietersen, dug in today to frustrate us from what we hoped would be a Test victory in four days. They batted with the sort of resolve we came to expect last time we met and while it wasn't unexpected, they are still in the contest come day five.

Paul Collingwood has the street-fighter qualities I admire in a sportsman and I felt his innings today was outstanding. On the other hand, Pietersen is also a

TAKE COVER: Pietersen does his best to avoid a short one

BEST MATES?: Kevin exchanges views with Shane

huge competitor who you would love to play with but don't particularly like playing against. He is a supreme talent with an equal quantity of self belief with a cricket bat in his hand. Both of these players are danger men in this series because of their skill and combative instincts.

Earlier in the day I was lucky to experience one of those magic moments that make all the dark times worthwhile. On ninety-nine and with an improving Steve Harmison running in at me, my

heart was pumping like a runaway train.

Thankfully I was able to control these nerves and push a single on to the leg-side to bring up my hundred. As I ran down the wicket I couldn't stop pumping my arms towards my team-mates. The joy was exhilarating and while it is hard to clearly define with words, this feeling is why we play the game. All of the hard work, physically and mentally, comes down to these rare moments on the cricket field.

View from the Boundary

Monday
27 November 2006

FIRST TEST, DAY FIVE

England began the day with the enormous and unlikely task of seeing out the full three sessions to secure a draw from this game but, in just the first over from Brett Lee, Kevin Pietersen, who had batted so superbly for his 92 clipped a full length delivery off his pads straight to the quick-reacting hands of Damien Martyn at short mid-wicket.

It was the worst possible start for England and it brought Giles to the crease to partner Jones.

Both then knuckled down for the next half an hour, with Giles in particular playing some attractive shots but, soon enough, a ball that kept a little low from McGrath took the inside edge of Jones's bat as he attempted to drive the ball on the up through the off-side, deflecting it into his middle stump for an encouraging 33.

Now well into the tail, Australia continued to apply pressure to the

NOT IN GOOD SHAPE: Geraint Jones gets a little out of position to a McGrath delivery and pays the price

England batsmen and, bowling with great control, Clark drew a false shot from Giles that caught the edge and presented an easy chance to Warne at first slip for a well made 23.

A BIG HAND: Hoggard thanks the Barmy Army for their unwavering support

Hoggard and Harmison now playing for pride as much as anything else, looked to score some

personal points against the Australian bowling attack with a collection of lusty blows before Hoggard too fell victim to an out-swinging delivery that he was looking to drive through cover and provided Warne with his second simple catch in as many overs.

Finally, it was Harmison who was the last man to go. Attempting to pull a shortish delivery from Clark, he top edged the stroke down to wide fine leg into the safe hands of McGrath to complete the England defeat just 10 minutes before lunch.

FIRST BLOOD TO US: McGrath and team-mates celebrate the match-winning wicket of Harmison

Monday
27 November 2006

FIRST TEST, DAY FIVE

Losing KP early without adding to his score was the last start we wanted and I felt sorry for him because we all wanted him to get a hundred under his belt. But there was more batting to come and Geraint Jones looked in terrific form making 33. I'm a bit one-eyed and biased where Geraint is concerned because he is one of my best mates in the team. Like Colly, he is a great scrapper and a very good player. We are lucky to have two very talented wicket-keepers in him and Chris Read

Ashley Giles also weighed in with a few runs and showed how much we have missed him during his spell out of the game with injury. To have him back and fit is a major boost to us and lengthens our batting line-up. Both he and Monty Panesar are fine bowlers, but for a series like this Ash is that bit more streetwise, which counts for a lot. Monty is an attacking bowler who looks to take wickets all the time, but when the pressure is on and the ball starts to fly about a bit Ash's experience is invaluable. He also gives the batsmen confidence coming in at eight. When the Flintoffs and Pietersens see a bowler coming in at that stage they start to think of opening up and accelerating. But with Ash there they have that bit more confidence to keep playing the same way. It also has to be said he is a terrific team player. For me, he was the right selection for this game and I welcomed him back with open arms.

I finished the game with my lobbed in the air pull shot, which was collected by Glenn McGrath. I was disappointed because I'm normally okay with that shot, but I'd got 13 and managed to play some nice shots off Warney so there was something positive to take from the innings. At the end of the day we were never going to save the match, but I felt it was a poor ball to get out to. It probably summed up the game as far as I was concerned.

We had been soundly beaten. When I got back to the hotel I looked in the mirror and said 'ten out of ten for effort, but nought out of ten for ability and performance.' Everything I tried, I gave 100 per cent to, but nothing worked out. No team can afford to carry passengers in an Ashes Test and I had been the biggest passenger of all in a very disappointing England performance. Inevitably, I took a lot of stick in the media and, while a lot of it was fair comment, some of it was personal or involved taking the mickey. There were suddenly a lot of experts on fast bowling and a lot of experts on Steve Harmison. I took in some of the criticism and rejected other parts of it.

BEGINNING OF THE END: Lee celebrates the prize wicket of Pietersen

As far as I am concerned there is still more than enough time for me to emerge a hero from this series.

1-0: Clark greets his keeper in celebration of Harmison's wicket

Monday
27 November 2006

FIRST TEST, DAY FIVE

Arriving at the ground on days like these there are always a few lingering doubts about whether you can actually finish off the job and deposit a Test victory into the bank.

Thoughts like, what if it rains? What if Pietersen hangs around and bats all day? What if the England tail wags?

These worries nag away until incidents like the second ball of the morning, when Pietersen hit a leg stump half volley from Brett Lee straight into the hands of Damien Martyn at short mid-wicket.

From that moment we knew the game would be ours and, although it took over an hour to complete the job, we walked off the Gabba satisfied that the job had been done, and done well.

Often after a Test victory of such magnitude the celebrations within the Australian changing room tend to be a raucous affair.

This wasn't the case today as we are well aware that there is still an enormous amount of hard work to do if we are to take back the Ashes.

Sitting in the rooms felt like sitting at base camp at the bottom of Mount Everest.

It is one thing being comfortable at base camp but in only four days we start our ascent up our current Mount Everest which is winning this series.

There is still a long way to go and while we are exhausted after five hot, humid and emotional days here in Queensland, the beautiful Adelaide Oval beckons and it is time to saddle up again for round two.

NOT AS WE PLANNED: Flintoff shares a moment with Jones

Brisbane

Adelaide

Perth

Melbourne

Sydney

Scorecard

Australia 1st Innings

			Runs	Balls	4s	6s
J L Langer	c K P Pietersen	b A Flintoff	**82**	98	13	0
M L Hayden	c K P Pietersen	b A Flintoff	**21**	47	2	0
R T Ponting	lbw	b M J Hoggard	**196**	319	24	0
D R Martyn	c P D Collingwood	b A F Giles	**29**	62	2	0
M E K Hussey		b A Flintoff	**86**	187	8	0
M J Clarke	c A J Strauss	b J M Anderson	**56**	94	5	1
A C Gilchrist	lbw	b M J Hoggard	**0**	3	0	0
S K Warne	c G O Jones	b S J Harmison	**17**	26	1	0
B Lee	not out		**43**	61	6	0
S R Clark		b A Flintoff	**39**	23	3	2
G D McGrath	not out		**8**	17	0	0
Extras		7nb 8w 2b 8lb	**25**			
Total		for 9	**602**	(155.0 ovs)		

Bowling	O	M	R	W
S J Harmison	30	4	123	1
M J Hoggard	31	5	98	2
J M Anderson	29	6	141	1
A Flintoff	30	4	99	4
A F Giles	25	2	91	1
I R Bell	1	0	12	0
K P Pietersen	9	1	28	0

Fall of wicket

79 (M L Hayden), 141 (J L Langer), 198 (D R Martyn), 407 (M E K Hussey), 467 (R T Ponting), 467 (A C Gilchrist), 500 (S K Warne), 528 (M J Clarke), 578 (S R Clark)

England 1st Innings

			Runs	Balls	4s	6s
A J Strauss	c M E K Hussey	b G D McGrath	**12**	21	2	0
A N Cook	c S K Warne	b G D McGrath	**11**	15	1	0
I R Bell	c R T Ponting	b S R Clark	**50**	162	5	0
P D Collingwood	c A C Gilchrist	b S R Clark	**5**	13	1	0
K P Pietersen	lbw	b G D McGrath	**16**	44	1	0
A Flintoff	c A C Gilchrist	b B Lee	**0**	3	0	0
G O Jones	lbw	b G D McGrath	**19**	57	2	0
A F Giles	c M L Hayden	b G D McGrath	**24**	39	4	0
M J Hoggard	c A C Gilchrist	b S R Clark	**0**	6	0	0
S J Harmison	c A C Gilchrist	b G D McGrath	**0**	5	0	0
J M Anderson	not out		**2**	8	0	0
Extras		6nb 2w 2b 8lb	**18**			
Total		all out	**157**	(61.1 ovs)		

Bowling	O	M	R	W
B Lee	15	3	51	1
G D McGrath	23.1	8	50	6
S R Clark	14	5	21	3
S K Warne	9	0	25	0

Fall of wicket

28 (A J Strauss), 28 (A N Cook), 42 (P D Collingwood), 78 (K P Pietersen), 79 (A Flintoff), 126 (G O Jones), 149 (I R Bell), 153 (M J Hoggard), 154 (S J Harmison), 157 (A F Giles)

Australia 2nd Innings

			Runs	Balls	4s	6s
J L Langer	not out		100	146	10	0
M L Hayden	run out		37	41	6	0
R T Ponting	not out		60	85	4	0
Extras		1nb 4lb	5			
Total		for 1	**202**		(45.1 ovs)	

Bowling	O	M	R	W
M J Hoggard	11	2	43	0
J M Anderson	9	1	54	0
A Flintoff	5	2	11	0
S J Harmison	12.1	1	54	0
A F Giles	5	0	22	0
K P Pietersen	3	0	14	0

Fall of wicket

68 (M L Hayden)

England 2nd Innings

			Runs	Balls	4s	6s
A J Strauss	c sub	b S R Clark	11	31	1	0
A N Cook	c M E K Hussey	b S K Warne	43	94	4	0
I R Bell	lbw	b S K Warne	0	4	0	0
P D Collingwood	c A C Gilchrist	b S K Warne	96	155	13	2
K P Pietersen	c D R Martyn	b B Lee	92	156	14	0
A Flintoff	c J L Langer	b S K Warne	16	26	4	0
G O Jones		b G D McGrath	33	47	5	0
A F Giles	c S K Warne	b S R Clark	23	38	3	0
M J Hoggard	c S K Warne	b S R Clark	8	35	1	0
S J Harmison	c G D McGrath	b S R Clark	13	18	2	0
J M Anderson	not out		4	8	1	0
Extras		11nb 2w 8b 10lb	31			
Total		all out	**370**		(100.1 ovs)	

Bowling	O	M	R	W
B Lee	22	1	98	1
G D McGrath	19	3	53	1
S R Clark	24.1	6	72	4
S K Warne	34	7	124	4
M E K Hussey	1	0	5	0

Fall of wicket

29 (A J Strauss), 36 (I R Bell), 91 (A N Cook), 244 (P D Collingwood), 271 (A Flintoff), 293 (K P Pietersen), 326 (G O Jones), 346 (A F Giles), 361 (M J Hoggard), 370 (S J Harmison)

Australia beat England by 277 runs

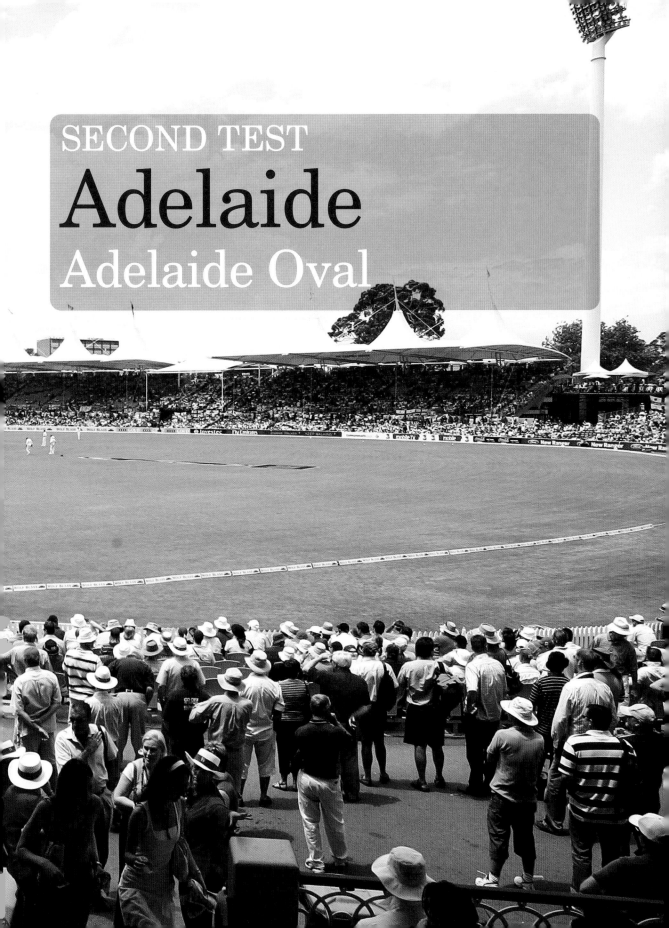

SECOND TEST
Adelaide
Adelaide Oval

View from the Boundary

Teams

Umpires: S A Bucknor, R E Koertzen

Australia: J L Langer, M L Hayden, R T Ponting, D R Martyn, M E K Hussey, M J Clarke, A C Gilchrist, S K Warne, B Lee, S R Clark, G D McGrath

England: A J Strauss, A N Cook, I R Bell, P D Collingwood, K P Pietersen, A Flintoff, G O Jones, A F Giles, M J Hoggard, S J Harmison, J M Anderson

England won the toss and elected to bat

Friday

01 December 2006

SECOND TEST, DAY ONE

England had the best possible news before the start of this crucial Test match when Flintoff saw the umpire's special Australian silver dollar land on his predicted side.

Freddie had no hesitation in asking the Australians to bowl on what is regarded as one of the flattest batting tracks in the country.

England, knowing the importance of setting Ricky Ponting's men a large first-innings total, began their innings very watchfully with both Strauss and Cook desperate to get their team off to a good start.

Perhaps a little too cautious on what appeared, on first inspection, to be a true and fairly slow batting surface, both openers progressed slowly through the first hour amassing just 30 runs. McGarth and Lee bowled their customary tight line but received little help from the pitch.

It wasn't until the introduction of Clark into the attack that England began to look uncomfortable against his persistent line and varying pace. After an opening stand of just 32 runs Strauss again contributed to his own downfall. In attempting to turn a ball through mid wicket he arrived a little early on the shot to a ball that was probably just short of a good length. The result was a mistimed chip to Martyn at short mid-on for a well judged catch.

With the arrival of Bell at the crease Ricky Ponting immediately brought Warne into the attack and, as is so often the case, he quickly found a probing line and a fair degree of turn for a first day surface. Bell, keen to be positive against his nemesis, made good use of his feet but was often found out by Warne's mixture of deliveries.

Just 2 overs after the dismissal of Strauss and with only 45 on the board, Cook too fell victim to the accurate and subtle variations of Clark's bowling. Driving on the up to a ball that was perhaps a little too wide to do so, resulted only in offering the simplest of nicks to the awaiting gloves of Gilchrist for a disappointing 27.

England, now fearful that they were squandering the opportunity this pitch was offering them, saw Collingwood, following his gritty innings at the Gabba, look to be

FINDING IT TOUGH GOING: Strauss avoids a quick delivery with the new ball

positive from the outset and by lunch both had survived to take England past fifty.

The 2 hours after lunch brought about the first wicket-less session of the series for England as Collingwood and Bell fought hard to ensure that the England 1st innings was on target for a satisfactory amount.

Both players, having picked up the pace a little since the break went into the interval on 50 n.o.

Shortly after the tea break, Bell, who had made an accomplished 60, was tempted to hook a fast-paced delivery from Lee that was a little outside off stump and managed only to top edge it straight up into the air for Lee to take a comfortable return catch.

That brought the danger man for Australia to the crease and he certainly lived up to his name.

Looking to be aggressive at every opportunity Pietersen quickly began scoring at a run a ball on his way to his second fifty of the series.

Meanwhile Collingwood, who was also looking to keep the scoreboard ticking over moved swiftly into the 90s playing both the old and new

ball with equal confidence.

At stumps England could be well satisfied with their day's effort. After a tricky start they had, through the efforts of the middle order, progressed to a very respectable 266-3 with Collingwood on the brink of a well-deserved century.

BACK INTO BATTLE: Collingwood looks to continue his good form from Brisbane

Brisbane

Adelaide

Perth

Melbourne

Sydney

Sydney

Melbourne

Perth

Adelaide

Brisbane

Friday
01 December 2006

SECOND TEST, DAY ONE

After a quiet day yesterday completing preparations – I just had a light bowling session and did my drills – we arrived at the Adelaide ground in good spirits and ready to put right the wrongs of the first Test. We had talked about the fact that we had kept the Australians in the field for a long time at the end of the Brisbane Test and felt if we could win the toss here we could bat again and exert more pressure on their physical fitness. Freddie did the business with the coin and, as the pitch was flat, that was a massive boost. We were coming off the back of a good hiding, but suddenly it was 'we've won the toss and here we go'. After losing a couple of early wickets, which you can always do to the new ball, we took control of the day thanks to some great batting by Ian Bell, Paul Collingwood and KP. The new ball

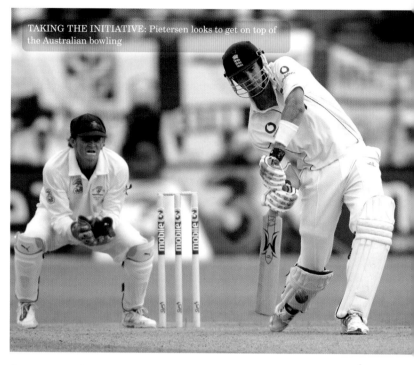

TAKING THE INITIATIVE: Pietersen looks to get on top of the Australian bowling

GOOD CALL: Flintoff wins the toss and bats

does swing and has a massive seam, but once it gets softer and the shine disappears it's tough for the pace bowlers and we knew we had the quality in our batting line-up to capitalise on that. I thought we did it remarkably well.

Their bowlers were on cloud nine after the first Test, but today we had them reeling. We ended the day 266-3, which we were very pleased with. We took a bit of stick for slow scoring and batting negatively, but Shane Warne, the best bowler ever to have played the game in my view, was reduced to going around the wicket to contain Kev, and KP had one of his heads on that was saying I'm not going to get beaten by this guy. The outfield was slow and our 266 was probably worth 300 or even 320 on another ground.

We didn't have the best of first sessions, losing those two early wickets, and didn't race away as we would like to have done. But the priority was to get ourselves back

into the series and to do that we needed a good first day.

There was a scare off the penultimate delivery when KP went for a big shot and the ball dropped just out of reach of McGrath at mid-off. When the ball is newer and the bowling a bit quicker his natural reaction is to increase his bat speed and things do happen. So we were sitting there watching the final deliveries of the day and thinking 'Oh my God, what's going to happen here'.

KP took some stick for the shot when he got back to the dressing room, but said he knew he was safe because McGrath was under it!

With KP safely not out overnight, we had consolidated our innings and Colly and Kev had laid the foundation for a massive partnership. The fighting qualities of the England team had come out after what happened at Brisbane and we went to bed well satisfied with our day's work.

in Adelaide and after a long day in the field today we will have to dismiss Collingwood, Pietersen and Flintoff early tomorrow if we are to stay in the game. The pitch was a perfect batting track today but as time goes on it is sure to deteriorate and get harder to score runs on.

Friday
01 December 2006

SECOND TEST, DAY ONE

Before the series began I mentioned to a few of my team-mates that I thought Paul Collingwood could be one of the danger men for England. His street-fighting instincts mean he is up for a scrap; an attitude that is sure to serve him well in the rough and tumble of Test cricket.

Today he fought hard from the moment he reached the crease and while he has to spend the night stuck on 98, he is proving something of a thorn in our side. After batting well in Brisbane he proved just as hard to remove today and unless we can get him out early in the morning he will take his country into a position of strength.

There is no doubt the toss of the coin can be a significant factor here

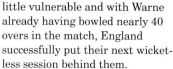

Saturday

02 December 2006

SECOND TEST, DAY TWO

England resumed their innings this morning with an important session ahead of them. At 266-3 both batsmen knew the importance of continuing their partnership if they were to take England into a comfortable position for their following team-mates.

Collingwood, who had battled so brilliantly through the first day, was delighted to grab the two remaining runs he needed to secure his first Test century against the old enemy and, seeing his partner's obvious intent to dominate, on reaching three figures he was happy to play supporting role to Kevin's flamboyance.

Pietersen, aggressive and on occasions dismissive, moved swiftly into the nineties with a collection of shots, orthodox and otherwise, that lifted both the run rate and spirit of the England innings.

Australia, anxious to make the breakthrough, managed to reign his scoring in a little as he neared the century mark but, still 45 minutes from lunch, Pietersen, with customary jubilation, pumped his arms to the delighted English fans and dressing room as he drove a quick single off Clark to claim his first ton of the tour.

With a partnership of over 150 under their belt, both players continued to look focused as they neared the interval and, with the slightly injured McGrath looking a

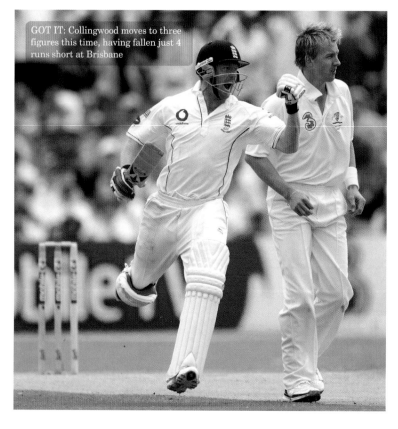

GOT IT: Collingwood moves to three figures this time, having fallen just 4 runs short at Brisbane

little vulnerable and with Warne already having bowled nearly 40 overs in the match, England successfully put their next wicket-less session behind them.

After lunch saw England begin to hammer home their advantage. Both batting with purpose and controlled aggression, Pietersen and Collingwood began to compile what was to become England's highest ever fourth-wicket partnership against Australia. Warne, now well over 100 runs against his name and without a wicket, chose a defensive line in an attempt to ensure England's innings was at least stalled in its progression.

After nearly three sessions together Collingwood struck Warne high over mid-on to record a fantastic double century. In a series where he was unlikely to have been picked for the Test side, were it not for the absence of Trescothick,

Sydney

Melbourne

Perth

Adelaide

Brisbane

NOT AGAIN: Pietersen fails to make his ground and is dismissed on 158 for the third time in his career

magnificent 206 and finally brought to a close a partnership worth an enormous 310 runs.

Following the break Pietersen took on an unlikely single to an alert Ricky Ponting and was run out for a formidable 158, the third such score of his career.

Jones, now at the crease with Flintoff and looking to progress the total quickly as the day drew to a close, finally gave Warne his much awaited first wicket of the innings, caught at backward point by Martyn.

It was then left to Flintoff and the ever reliable Giles to take the total past 550, at which point, and with just 30 minutes of the day remaining, Freddie decided it was time to have a short spell at the field-weary opposition.

Electing to open the bowling with himself and Hoggard, Freddie's decision was soon to prove a good one with early wicket of Langer, caught in the gulley for 4 by Pietersen from a delivery that rose steeply off a length.

Australia, facing an awkward nine overs before the close, were able to see out the day without further loss to finish on 28-1.

Collingwood had completed over 300 runs in his first 3 innings of the tour. Pietersen too, with ever increasing maturity, complimented the sporadic aggression of his partner to bring up his 150.

On the stroke of tea however, Collingwood finally fell victim to the in-form Clark. Driving a full-length ball that was a little too wide, he edged a simple chance to Gilchrist behind the stumps for a

GOOD SUPPORT: Giles backs up his captain with a well-made 27

Brisbane

Adelaide

Perth

Melbourne

Sydney

Steve Harmison

Saturday

02 December 2006

SECOND TEST, DAY TWO

I've known Paul Collingwood since 1996 so to see him score a double century against Australia today gave me a huge amount of pleasure.

Colly has come a long, long way since he first arrived on the Test Match scene. A couple of times he has got into the nervous nineties and thrown his wicket away with a rush of blood. So the one thing I will always remember about his innings in this match was the way he went to 200. It wasn't the shot as much as the whoop of joy you could hear when he got to the pitch of the ball from Shane Warne and smashed it away for four.

That typifies Colly and the way he plays the game. As a fellow Durham lad, I was thrilled for him. He has proved to everyone what a fighter and a good character he is. I'm sure it helped him having KP at the other end for so long because it enabled him to knock the ball around in the couple of periods where he got bogged down a bit. Colly's problem earlier in his career was that he got pigeon-holed as a 'bits and pieces cricketer' and nobody really talked about him as an out and out batsman. Those of us who worked with him day in day out at Durham knew he was more than a number seven who bowled seamers, and that being deemed an all-rounder wasn't doing him any good. He is now the best fielder in world cricket in my opinion and has shown his quality as a batsman at the highest level.

He has been a fighter all his career to get to where he is and now he is a fantastic team player for England. He was chuffed to bits with his innings today, but Colly will have a smile on his face whether he has scored 200 or nought. He's one of those lads who is never down for long and great to have in the dressing room. The only time you see him down is when someone takes money off him on the golf course – and that doesn't happen often!

Kevin Pietersen was out for 158. No surprise there because he always gets out on 158! – the lads couldn't avoid a few chuckles when the old hoodoo struck again. KP was laughing himself as he walked off because he just couldn't believe it. In the dressing room he was disappointed not to have gone on to an even bigger score, but I wouldn't mind getting out on 158 a few times!

We declared on 551-6 to give the Aussies a tricky short session to bat at the end of the day and managed to get Justin Langer out to leave them 28-1 overnight. Freddie had his tail up and got a ball to bounce a bit at Langer, which was a good effort on this pitch. I didn't get to bowl in the short session and faced a further wait to try and put the demons of Brisbane behind me. But the team left the field with a spring in our step and seeing this as a game we could really get hold of.

ENGLAND		
1ST INNINGS		
2ND INNINGS		
AUSTRALIA		
1ST INNINGS		
2ND INNINGS		
WICKETS		4
PIETERSEN	1	4 6
· COLLINGW'D	2	0 6
SUNDRIES		1 4
TOTAL	4	6 8

ASHES *frontline*

Saturday
02 December 2006

SECOND TEST, DAY TWO

The night before the first Test I was sitting on Shane Warne's hotel balcony with a couple of the guys. We were discussing the upcoming series and I predicted one of the players we had to be wary of was Paul Collingwood. For a while it took them some convincing but my rationale was that he had fighting instincts that could wind us up and stand him in good stead to succeed in Test cricket.

With a 96 in Brisbane and a double century today it would be fair to say my concerns have been validated. He is a gutsy player who obviously knows his game and plays it accordingly. We will have to re-visit our plans regarding him if we are to nullify his impact for the remainder of the series.

As for Kevin Pietersen, he played some of the most amazing shots I have ever seen on a cricket field. He is a brilliant batsman who hits the ball as pure as anyone I have played against. He is another one on whom we will need to do some more homework before the next time he bats.

After eleven and a half hours in the field we had to bat for forty minutes and ten overs before stumps today. Such occasions are the only thing I dislike about opening the batting, especially when you lose your wicket. The bowlers are fired up with nothing to lose while we have to face the fire with very little to gain. Historically it has been rare for me to get out in these testing periods but today I was caught off a rising ball from Freddie Flintoff. It was interesting to see him opening the bowling. There has been plenty of speculation about whether he would take the new ball after Brisbane and today he did just that; with some success, which happened to be my failure.

The irony as an opening batsman is that when you get through these times it is a very satisfying feeling and yet when you don't the whole world turns blue. Tomorrow is another interesting day where we will have to bat for as long as we can.

THIS ONE'S MINE: Collingwood, having been out to Warne in Brisbane, lifts a flighted delivery high over mid-on to bring up his double century

RESTORING SOME PRIDE: England batsmen Collingwood and Pietersen leave the field after a record-breaking partnership

Brisbane

Adelaide

Perth

Melbourne

Sydney

HOW MUCH WILL THAT COST?: Giles ponders the consequences of dropping Ponting on 32

Australia were now 65-3 and facing an uphill task to match the tourists' first-innings total and, soon after the dismissal of Martyn, Ponting, who had been tied to the crease for some time, pulled at a ball that got up quite high off a full length and sent a fast chance to Giles on the boundary at deep square leg. Giles though, perhaps deceived by the ball's pace failed to hold on to the chance and, although certainly England's session, an opportunity had been missed as they neared the lunch break.

Following a good start to the day England were made to pay for their missed catch. Ricky Ponting, like all of the world's best batsmen, is not a man to give a second chance to and he, along with his partner

A HIGH PRICE INDEED: Ponting is finally dismissed for a magnificent 142

Sunday

03 December 2006

SECOND TEST, DAY THREE

As Mark Taylor put it "England appear to have changed jumpers with their opponents for this Test match".

Bowling with superb accuracy and tight control England began the day with great focus, looking to bowl with a plan to each of the Australian batsmen.

Mathew Hayden, who had fallen victim to his temptation outside the off stump on previous occasions, was to find himself being drawn in again to an out-swinger from

Hoggard and, in attempting to drive the Yorkshireman through cover, got a thick edge through to Jones for just 12.

Ponting too, for a man in superb form, was being held at the crease by a consistent approach from all four of England's seamers.

Martyn, who looked in good touch, was the next to fall victim to this disciplined attack. Reaching out to another out-swinger from Hoggard, he pushed a well-timed two through cover. Hoggard, then skilfully quickening his pace for the same delivery, got Martyn reaching for another, only this time, in playing too far from his body, the ball caught a thick edge and was brilliantly picked up by Bell in the gulley.

Sydney

Melbourne

Perth

Adelaide

Brisbane

Michael Hussey, dug in to bring the Australian innings back on track.

England, continuing to bowl with control and a positive spirit, were successful however in keeping the hosts' run-rate to a sensible level but, as the session progressed, both players offered little in the way of chances as Hussey moved towards 50 and Ponting towards another century.

In the penultimate over before tea, Ponting snatched a single off Flintoff to record his 32nd century of his career, the most by any Australian, and ensure that this session had been a successful one for his team.

After tea produced a similar style of play from both teams. England continued to probe at the batsmen with a controlled line and length whilst Australia, in defiant mood, progressed the score at a steady rate.

It wasn't until the last hour of play, with 257 on the board and a partnership of 192 under their belts, that Ponting on 142 was drawn into a good-length ball from Hoggard that shaped away a little and took a thin edge through to Jones to bring Clarke to the middle.

England, sensing that a couple of wickets at this stage of the day would hand the honours to them, pressured hard and with Hussey just nine runs short of his century, it was Hoggard again who, with a consistent line on his off stump, drew a little uncertainly from the batsman and, in attempting to draw his bat out of the way of one he need not have played, he caught the ball with the toe of his bat and deflected it into the path of his off stump. It was Hoggard's fourth wicket of the day and just reward for an excellent spell of bowling.

Gilchrist now joined Clarke at the crease to see out a tense last 20 minutes but, following on from his duck at the Gabba and keen to get a big score to his name against the tourists, he looked confident, timing the ball well up until the end of play.

ONE NOT TO LEAVE: Hussey looks with dismay as he falls short of a deserved century

Brisbane

Adelaide

Perth

Melbourne

Sydney

EDGING SLIGHTLY IN FRONT: The England team congratulate Hoggard after Hussey plays one onto his stumps

Steve Harmison

Sunday
03 December 2006

SECOND TEST, DAY THREE

This was Matthew Hoggard's day. While Freddie, Jimmy Anderson and I toiled away, Hoggy seemed to be bowling on a different pitch. It was a great bit of bowling.

He set Matthew Hayden up brilliantly by bringing three or four balls back into him and then ran one across him and did pretty much the same to Damian Martyn. I felt I bowled a couple of tight overs at Martyn and when Hoggy has given him a wide one he's nicked it straight to gully. I felt we bowled well as a team on a flat, flat wicket. All five of us bowled in good areas and kept to our plan, even though we didn't get the rewards we might have.

My first ball of the day came after several overs had been bowled and to say I was nervous would be putting it politely. I've run up and let go of the ball and seen it pitch in

IN THE SWING OF THINGS: Hoggard celebrates the early wicket of Hayden.

a good area. Just what I wanted after Brisbane. Next ball I've run up and done the same and then Freddie has come over to talk about moving an extra fielder into a catching position. I looked at him and said: "No, no, I can't think about that at the moment. Just let me get through the next couple of balls and I'll be alright." All I wanted to focus on was getting the over completed, which sums up how Brisbane had affected me.

That first over went well and all day I felt I was bowling in good areas. I just needed a wicket and it didn't come. I was searching for it and the one thing I probably did wrong was to strive that little bit too hard for it. That was disappointing, but I came off the field happy because I had bowled at the top side of 92mph and maintained decent accuracy.

A big moment of the day was when Ashley Giles dropped Ricky Ponting off Hoggy with his score on 35. Again it was a great bit of bowling by Hoggy, who had been dragging Ponting forward for a couple of overs and suddenly banged one in short, which he didn't quite pick up. When he failed to make proper contact with his pull shot I straight away thought 'yes, he's out' because the ball was heading for Ash, who is one of the best catchers in the team, and it looked as thought it was going to him waist-high, however the ball didn't come down. It just kept going and going and going. In the end it has been a difficult catch above his head, but one Ash will be very disappointed not to have taken. No one drops catches on purpose and we had to move on, but it was obviously a costly one as Ricky went on to score 142.

Australia ended the day 312-5 and we still felt in full control of the game.

ASHES *frontline*

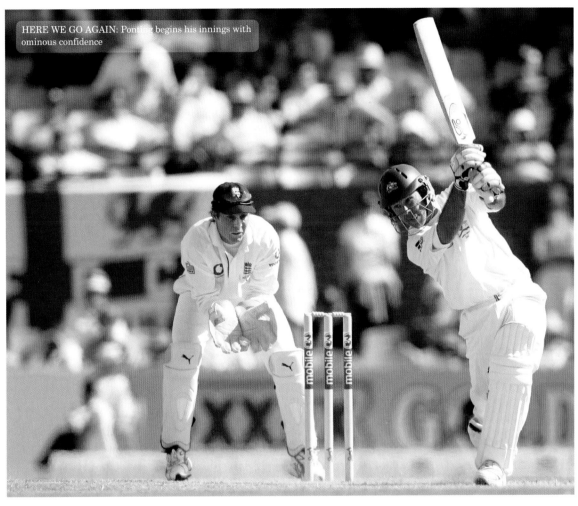

HERE WE GO AGAIN: Ponting begins his innings with ominous confidence

Sunday
03 December 2006

SECOND TEST, DAY THREE

In Ricky Ponting the cricket world is witnessing something special. After another magnificent century, his 33rd in Test cricket, he helped steady the ship to put us back within reach of England. The mind boggles how the little master can keep churning out the runs like he does. With the extra pressures associated with batting at number three and captaining the side, he is without doubt one of the mentally toughest people I know.

His average since taking over the captaincy is exceptional and it is little wonder he is being described as the next best batsman to Sir Donald Bradman.

Not only do the statistics back up these claims but the way he goes about his job suggests he is nearly impossible to bowl to. A little short and he will hook, pull or cut the bowler to the square boundary, a fraction full and he will pounce onto his front foot and smash it straight down the ground or through mid-wicket and the covers. The man is a genius and is the best player I have ever seen, along with Sachin and B C Lara.

The captain's effort with Michael Hussey was crucial for us in this Test match and if we are to have any chance of an improbable victory then we will need a similar partnership from Michael Clark and Adam Gilchrist tomorrow.

For England Matthew Hoggard bowled brilliantly today, while Steve Harmison looked to have found some rhythm; a worrying sign for us going forward in the series.

View from the Boundary

Monday
04 December 2006

SECOND TEST, DAY FOUR

Both teams began what is probably the most important session of this Test match so far. With the game delicately poised, Australia were looking to bring themselves up to parity with England keen to establish a first-innings lead.

England began well with more of the consistent line and length that had proved successful to date. Realising that this Adelaide pitch required a conservative and accurate approach, Hoggard and Flintoff restricted the hosts to just 13 runs in the first 40 minutes.

Then, with the arrival of Giles, Harmison and Anderson into the attack, Gilchrist began to open his shoulders. Having timed the ball well since the start of his innings,

Gilchrist had moved comfortably to 30 but now began to show the sort of form that had terrorised bowling attacks across the world. Within a matter of moments, ably assisted by Clarke who moved steadily to his second fifty of the series at the other end, he raced past fifty and began to turn the momentum of this game towards Australia. However, with 64 on the board, he attempted to sweep Giles over mid-wicket and, slightly mistiming the stroke, presented a comfortable waist-high catch to Bell moving in from the deep.

That brought Warne to the crease and with it, a sense of opportunity and relief for England. With a combination of Pietersen and Harmison, Flintoff attempted to tease the newcomer into something rash but, with typical nerve, Warne and Clarke saw their team through to the break.

After lunch both Warne and Clarke appeared immovable objects

as England persevered, with plenty of variation on this placid pitch, without success.

Clarke, eager to cement his place in the team, played faultlessly and, supported well by Warne, who was checking his normal temptation to be extravagant, took himself to the magical three figures. In for the injured Watson, Clarke certainly provided his selectors with a headache in compiling a great innings under some pressure.

By the time the tea break neared, England would have been considering that a draw was the most likely outcome from this game.

Once Hoggard was back in the attack and getting a little reverse swing from the old ball, he first picked up the wicket of Warne, lbw for 43 and then just 3 runs later, claimed the centurion, caught by Giles for 124.

Now 505-8, a small first-innings lead was a possibility and, only

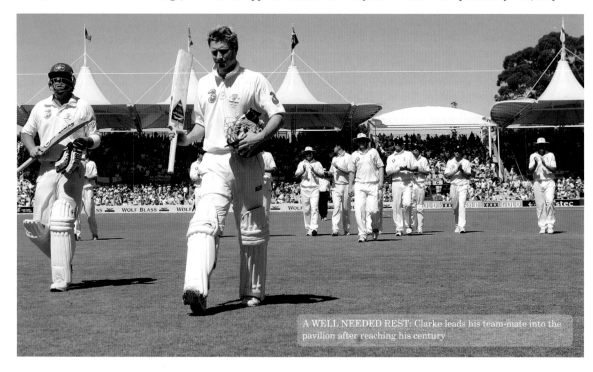

A WELL NEEDED REST: Clarke leads his team-mate into the pavilion after reaching his century

ASHES frontline

NOT OVER YET: Warne begins to apply pressure to the England top order

minutes later, looked more likely when Hoggard took his seventh wicket of the match by bowling the newcomer Clark, attempting to repeat his efforts from the Gabba.

Now with McGrath at the crease with Lee, Anderson was brought back into bowl with Flintoff hoping that his bowler's natural full length would bring about a miscued drive and, sure enough, it wasn't long before McGrath pushed outside off stump to one and sent a low catch through to Jones.

The Australians had now completed their innings 38 runs behind England's total, mainly due to the enormous workmanlike efforts of Hoggard, finishing on an Ashes best 7-109.

The odds in this game, given that the pitch is still playing well, point towards a draw, but both teams were looking to get something from the final 18 overs of the day.

Australia, with Warne certain to get great turn from this wearing surface, were anxious to take a few wickets before the close, both to prevent England building a quick lead and to provide themselves with an outside chance for victory.

Strauss, keen to get his first decent total of the tour, looked to be playing with great touch in the opening overs, paying considerable attention to keeping the ball down in the early part of his innings.

With Lee and McGrath posing few problems in their opening

spells captain Ricky Ponting turned to his most reliable of performers to make something happen. Warne immediately got the ball to grip out of the rough and, before long, had several players around the bat applying pressure to the openers.

However, it was Clark, bowling his accurate medium pacers at the other end, who was to strike first. Sending down a delivery that almost mirrored the one he bowled to dismiss Cook in the first innings, Cook responded in identical fashion and tentatively pushed at it, edging it through to Gilchrist for 9.

Bell came in to join Strauss and, with growing confidence, both men saw England through to stumps and a lead of 97.

Monday
04 December 2006

SECOND TEST, DAY FOUR

Although Australia have gone on to make 513 and got themselves back into the game with a deficit of only 38 on first innings, we felt we had bowled well again.

We didn't expect them to get 500 from their overnight position and perhaps we took the pressure off at times. Gilchrist looked nervy early on when we were putting the ball in good areas and then we released him a bit, while Michael Clarke has simply played well on a flat pitch for his century.

The ball wasn't doing anything and if you look at the bowling figures for the seamers on both sides in the respective first innings, Matthew Hoggard apart, you can see how tough it was for us – McGrath, Brett Lee, Stuart Clark, Freddie, Jimmy and myself all toiled without much reward. We just weren't in the game, but I still felt that as a team we had out-batted and out-bowled Australia in the two innings.

Hoggy finished with 7-109, which was an unbelievable and exceptional effort. He bowled to a plan with a good field set for him that allowed him freedom to try and make the ball swing. The balls swung for him when new and he kept putting his deliveries in the right area, with enough shape on them to dangle a carrot and find the edge. He was saying to the batsmen "Hit me, have a go for it". Hussey was another who fell to a great bit of bowling where Hoggy slanted the ball across him a few times and then brought one back.

You need a bit of luck when a batsman plays onto his stumps, but when you are in top form things tend to go for you. It was a fantastic effort by Hoggy. Without his seven wickets I think we might still be out there bowling now!

Again we lost an early wicket to the new ball in our second innings, but finishing the day on 59-1, with a lead of 87, is still a healthy position.

GAINING CONFIDENCE: Gilchrist, after an edgy start, begins to get into his stride

Monday
04 December 2006

SECOND TEST, DAY FOUR

Today Michael Clarke came of age as a Test batsman. After a meteoric rise a couple of years ago, he has sat in the wilderness, contemplating his Test cricket future. Like all of the crop of current Australian batsman, this time out of the team has proved to be a valuable period for him as he worked out where he had to improve and what he had to do to force another opportunity.

When that chance came in Brisbane last week he eked out a steady half century and looked like a boy who had conquered his early

SECURING HIS PLACE: Clarke, following a steady start in Brisbane, salutes the crowd on reaching a beautifully-crafted ton

LENDING SUPPORT: Warne backs up his team-mate with a well-made 43

haste of wanting to run before he had even crawled. Today, he took his progression a step further and in my mind is now set to run for as long as he wants in the baggy green cap. As unlikely as it may seem, his effort with Adam Gilchrist and Shane Warne in taking us so close to England's huge first-innings total, gives us a chance to pull off a remarkable victory.

There is only one winner in this game now and it is not the visitors. The pitch is deteriorating and while there is a mountain of work to do, you just never know in Test cricket. Matthew Hoggard showed that the ball is starting to reverse swing on the drying surface and the ball is sure to spin for Shane Warne. We can sense something special is still to come.

Brisbane

Adelaide

Perth

Melbourne

Sydney

View from the Boundary

Tuesday
05 December 2006

SECOND TEST, DAY FIVE

Australia began the day with a draw, the most likely outcome, but, within minutes, an unlikely victory seemed a possibility.

Having added just 10 runs to their overnight total, England lost Strauss to an unfortunate decision from the umpire, adjudging him to have hit a ball from Warne that bounced up off his pads to Hussey at short leg.

They might have been able to consider themselves unlucky for that but, what followed, was to be their fault entirely.

Warne, getting tremendous turn and bite from this Adelaide surface, now had a collection of fielders around the bat and, with the pressure showing on the England batsman, Bell hesitated in going for a quick single and, after having played well to 26, was easily run out by Clarke.

England, now having lost 2 wickets in the first few minutes of the day, were 70-3 as Pietersen strode to the crease. However, it wasn't long before they were another one down. Attempting to sweep a virtual full toss from Warne, Pietersen misjudged the flight and, in missing the ball, looked with horror as it bit, turned and bowled him around his legs.

Warne and the Australians reacted with obvious jubilation as the danger man in the England team was gone and, with a lead of just 111 runs, victory was becoming a probability.

Now with Flintoff and Collingwood in the middle, the captain again looked nervous as he attempted to steady his team's

ship. Looking to try and be positive, knowing that every run on the board was bringing his side closer to safety, Flintoff was drawn into playing a wide and inviting-looking delivery from Lee and, with a look of total despair saw his nick fly into the safe gloves of Gilchrist.

England were now an incredible 77-5 as Jones came to the middle and facing an enormous task to save this game and, with it, almost certainly, the series.

Looking focused and determined, both players, through a mixture of tremendous deliveries, loud appeals and a ball that was both turning and reverse swinging, managed to hang on until the break.

The next session was to produce an incredibly tense battle between bat and ball.

England, trying desperately to hang on under immense pressure from Warne and company, struggled to get a run as they battled with the sharp turn of Shane Warne and the vicious reverse swing that Lee was getting with the old ball.

Limping their way to 94, Jones was finally tempted by a very wide delivery from Lee and, hoping that he could release some pressure with a boundary, was drawn into a flashing drive wide of his off stump which flew to the right of Hayden for a good catch. Jones gone for just 10 and England now six down, Giles came to the middle to try and support Collingwood. He though, after just 3 runs had been added to the total, was to fall victim to the extra bounce and turn Warne was getting from this pitch, and edged a second catch to Hayden at slip for 0.

Now 97-7 and in deep trouble, Hoggard, who had bowled so well to keep England in this game, was now in the middle trying to save it. Collingwood, anxious that he was going to run out of partners, did his

best to keep strike but again, just 8 runs later, it was Warne who got the better of his man and bowled Hoggard off an inside edge for 4.

As the runs edged up slowly and, perhaps more importantly the overs were ticking away, England knew that if they could last until tea there was an outside chance of saving this game. Collingwood, who had batted for over a hundred deliveries and was yet to pass 20, was now partnered by Harmison.

Steve, not known for his defence, did his best to keep out the good balls and move the score on when possible but, on the return of the deadly accurate Glen McGrath, he was to fatefully leave a ball that came back in on him and was adjudged lbw for 8.

Now 119-9 and just one wicket away from disaster, England looked to try and bat out the remaining 40 minutes to the break. Anderson, looking as comfortable as one could in the situation and the ever-gritty

TURNING POINT: Pietersen gets bowled around his legs attempting to sweep a Warne delivery

restrict the flow of runs but, Hoggard, at a time when the pace of the game was already getting away from them, had Hayden pulling a ball that was a little too full and sent a skyer to Collingwood at square leg for a fantastic effort.

Now 33-2, England had a sniff of a chance but Giles, in the middle of a short spell of indifferent deliveries, could not find a satisfactory length bowling to a left and right hander, and both batsmen moved the scoring on at a steady rate.

Finally, after a partnership of 83 and, apart from the captain himself, no bowler looking like taking a wicket, Giles had Ponting driving outside the off stump to a ball that turned a little and, in doing so, sent it to the hands of Strauss for 49.

At 116-3, it was wickets alone that would bring about an unlikely saviour for England and, just five runs later, Flintoff got the wicket

he deserved when Martyn, looking to be aggressive from the moment he arrived in the middle and who had hit Flintoff for 4 over long off off his first delivery, was out-thought by his counterpart by a ball that was dug into him and, in attempting a drive off the back foot, was caught at slip by Strauss for 5.

Now 121-4, a slim chance had presented itself to England but Hussey, who looked in great touch and a resilient Clarke, both began to edge away at the target with little or no trouble.

With England's bowlers showing only sporadic form the total was soon to become too much for them, and with it faded the chances of a draw.

Finally, Hussey saw the Australians home with an unbeaten 61 and finish off what had been a most skilfully executed and most unlikely team victory.

Collingwood, pushed the score up to 129 before, on the very last ball before the break, Anderson walked across his stumps to a full delivery from McGrath and was given out lbw.

England had set Australia just 168 for victory from 36 overs.

Australia took the decision not to hang around in pursuing this small target. As a country they have an unfortunate record in falling short of small totals. England hung onto the hope that history would repeat itself.

Langer and Hayden both looked to get on with it and, after the first 2 overs, were already on 12 and ahead of the required rate of 4.66.

However, with the score on 14, Langer hit one out of the middle of the bat straight to Bell in the gulley and their first wicket was down.

Ponting joined Hayden and immediately looked in the same sort of form he had shown all series. Flintoff, changing his bowlers frequently, was struggling to find a team-mate who could

A BODY BLOW: Stunned England players leave the field to contemplate just what went wrong

Brisbane

Adelaide

Perth

Melbourne

Sydney

View from the Boundary

TAKING FLIGHT: Hussey lifts his arms in delight as he hits the winning runs for Australia

Brisbane

Adelaide

Perth

Melbourne

Sydney

Tuesday

05 December 2006

SECOND TEST, DAY FIVE

The plan at the start of the day was, let's get to lunch and see how we are placed then. Being realistic, we knew that unless there was a mad hour at the end, the game was heading for a draw.

Ideally, we wanted to extend our second innings to around 150 by lunch and then take the long handle to it for a while to leave the Aussies 250 or perhaps a bit more to make in around 45 overs. Then if we could knock four or five of their batsmen over, we could head to Perth for the third Test in the ascendancy.

We never like to whinge too much over umpiring decisions, but TV replays proved we got three dodgy ones today and the dismissal of Andrew Strauss was pivotal. Even so, there was no sense of panic in the dressing room at that point until a mad hour turned our quest for a moral victory into a backs-to-the-wall fight to save the game.

By the time I went in it was all about occupying the crease and using up time. I felt quite comfortable with Paul Collingwood at the other end and he told me we needed to bat for ten overs and then if Jimmy could come in and bat for ten overs too the game would be safe.

When McGrath started bowling Colly told me to play forward as far as possible to reduce the chance of an lbw. So I took guard fully a foot outside my crease and threw my front leg forward at everything. Glen swung three away from me and then brought one back in. But it only clipped the top of my pad and when I saw the finger go up I couldn't believe it. When Jimmy started to dig in with Colly it still seemed we would still save the game. Sadly, he got the third poor decision of the innings, lbw to a McGrath delivery that looked to be heading past leg stump, and we were all out.

Australia needed 168 to win at less than five an over. But before taking the field we talked about being nearer a winning position than we had been at 70-3 in our second innings because they still had to get the runs on a last-day pitch.

When we got both openers out with 33 on the board all three results were still possible. But the fast start by Langer and Hayden meant Ponting and Hussey could afford a little time to play themselves in. The pitch ruled out bowling any bouncers and after we

managed to get Ponting and Martyn out, Hussey and Clark knocked the ball around to seal victory.

In the dressing room afterwards the feeling was almost surreal. I just lay on the floor among my scattered kit just gazing at the ceiling and wondering how we could have lost having done so well for four days. We were the better team for that much of the match and one mad hour has cost us so dearly.

After pulling ourselves around as best we could, we packed our kit and headed to the Aussie dressing room where, if I'm honest, I stayed until one o'clock the next morning. Two hours after the match had finished, which is when we went in, things had calmed down a bit and I sensed the Australians were as disbelieving as we were over the result.

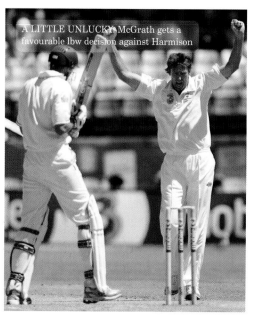

A LITTLE UNLUCKY McGrath gets a favourable lbw decision against Harmison

A MASTER CLASS: Warne lets out yet another appeal as he maintains enormous pressure on the tourists

Tuesday

05 December 2006

SECOND TEST, DAY FIVE

As predicted yesterday we could sense something special, but not in my wildest dreams could I have guessed at what transpired today. In thirteen years of Test cricket I can't remember a more remarkable victory.

When John Buchanan announced to the world that he was an optimist who believed Australia could still win this Test, you could almost hear the sniggers. The cynics may have thought he had lost his marbles and his retirement at the end of the World Cup was probably six months too late. What he knew, as did his eleven players, was that he had at his disposal a couple of masters of the game who are fiercely determined to win these Ashes.

Shane Warne showed once again why he is one of the greatest players to have ever played the game. The difference between the awesome successes of this team compared to others lies often in the brilliance of Warne. Today he entertained the world with pure competitive genius, while at the same time making a mockery of Duncan Fletcher's pre-Test prediction that England had taken an edge over the master.

Again our captain was fantastic in his tactics and batting prowess, while Michael Hussey continued his climb into the heady heights of international greatness. In his short career he is already forging a reputation as a man for the big occasion. When he cover drove the winning runs off James Anderson our changing room erupted into a sea of emotion.

From the moment the result was complete there was an overwhelming feeling that we had achieved something quite extraordinary. This was a masterful team performance led by two modern marvels of the game in Ricky and Shane, and now with two Test matches in the bank, we know the Ashes are within reach.

England will be bitterly disappointed and while both teams drank together well into the night, I am certain our hangovers will be much easier to cope with when the sun comes up in the morning.

IMMOVABLE OBJECT: Hussey salutes his dressing room as he passes yet another fifty

Scorecard

England 1st Innings

			Runs	Balls	4s	6s
A J Strauss	*c D R Martyn*	*b S R Clark*	**14**	44	0	0
A N Cook	*c A C Gilchrist*	*b S R Clark*	**27**	57	2	0
I R Bell	*c and b*	*B Lee*	**60**	148	6	0
P D Collingwood	*c A C Gilchrist*	*b S R Clark*	**206**	392	16	0
K P Pietersen	*run out*		**158**	257	15	1
A Flintoff	*run out*		**38**	67	2	1
G O Jones	*c D R Martyn*	*b S K Warne*	**1**	7	0	0
A F Giles	*not out*		**27**	44	4	0
Extras		*8nb 2w 10lb*	**20**			
Total		*for 6*	**551**	(168.0 ovs)		

Bowling	O	M	R	W
B Lee	34	1	139	1
G D McGrath	30	5	107	0
S R Clark	34	6	75	3
S K Warne	53	9	167	1
M J Clarke	17	2	53	0

Fall of wicket

32 (A J Strauss), 45 (A N Cook), 158 (I R Bell),
468 (P D Collingwood), 489 (K P Pietersen), 491 (G O Jones)

Australia 1st Innings

			Runs	Balls	4s	6s
J L Langer	*c K P Pietersen*	*b A Flintoff*	**4**	8	1	0
M L Hayden	*c G O Jones*	*b M J Hoggard*	**12**	30	1	0
R T Ponting	*c G O Jones*	*b M J Hoggard*	**142**	245	12	0
D R Martyn	*c I R Bell*	*b M J Hoggard*	**11**	33	1	0
M E K Hussey		*b M J Hoggard*	**91**	212	7	1
M J Clarke	*c A F Giles*	*b M J Hoggard*	**124**	224	10	0
A C Gilchrist	*c I R Bell*	*b A F Giles*	**64**	79	8	0
S K Warne	*lbw*	*b M J Hoggard*	**43**	108	4	0
B Lee	*not out*		**7**	33	0	0
S R Clark		*b M J Hoggard*	**0**	7	0	0
G D McGrath	*c G O Jones*	*b J M Anderson*	**1**	21	0	0
Extras		*7nb 1w 4b 2lb*	**14**			
Total		*all out*	**513**	(165.3 ovs)		

Bowling	O	M	R	W
M J Hoggard	42	6	109	7
A Flintoff	26	5	82	1
S J Harmison	25	5	96	0
J M Anderson	21.3	3	85	1
A F Giles	42	7	103	1
K P Pietersen	9	0	32	0

Fall of wicket

8 (J L Langer), 35 (M L Hayden), 65 (D R Martyn),
257 (R T Ponting), 286 (M E K Hussey), 384 (A C Gilchrist),
502 (S K Warne), 505 (M J Clarke), 507 (S R Clark),
513 (G D McGrath)

England 2nd Innings

			Runs	Balls	4s	6s
A J Strauss	c M E K Hussey	b S K Warne	34	79	3	0
A N Cook	c A C Gilchrist	b S R Clark	9	35	1	0
I R Bell	run out		26	73	2	0
P D Collingwood	not out		22	119	2	0
K P Pietersen		b S K Warne	2	5	0	0
A Flintoff	c A C Gilchrist	b B Lee	2	24	0	0
G O Jones	c M L Hayden	b B Lee	10	24	1	0
A F Giles	c M L Hayden	b S K Warne	0	8	0	0
M J Hoggard		b S K Warne	4	24	0	0
S J Harmison	lbw	b G D McGrath	8	21	0	0
J M Anderson	lbw	b G D McGrath	1	28	0	0
Extras		2nb 1w 3b 5lb	11			
Total		all out	129	(73.0 ovs)		

Bowling	O	M	R	W
B Lee	18	3	35	2
G D McGrath	10	6	15	2
S K Warne	32	12	49	4
S R Clark	13	4	22	1

Fall of wicket

31 (A N Cook), 69 (A J Strauss), 70 (I R Bell), 73 (K P Pietersen), 77 (A Flintoff), 94 (G O Jones), 97 (A F Giles), 105 (M J Hoggard), 119 (S J Harmison), 129 (J M Anderson)

Australia 2nd Innings

			Runs	Balls	4s	6s
J L Langer	c I R Bell	b M J Hoggard	7	8	1	0
M L Hayden	c P D Collingwood	b A Flintoff	18	17	2	0
R T Ponting	c A J Strauss	b A F Giles	49	65	5	0
M E K Hussey	not out		61	66	5	0
D R Martyn	c A J Strauss	b A Flintoff	5	4	1	0
M J Clarke	not out		21	39	0	0
Extras		2nb 1w 2b 2lb	7			
Total		for 4	168	(32.5 ovs)		

Bowling	O	M	R	W
M J Hoggard	4	0	29	1
A Flintoff	9	0	44	2
A F Giles	10	0	46	1
S J Harmison	4	0	15	0
J M Anderson	3.5	0	23	0
K P Pietersen	2	0	7	0

Fall of wicket

14 (J L Langer), 33 (M L Hayden), 116 (R T Ponting), 121 (D R Martyn)

Australia beat England by 6 wickets

THIRD TEST
Perth
The WACA

View from the Boundary

Teams

Umpires: Aleem Dar, R E Koertzen

Australia: M L Hayden, J L Langer, R T Ponting, M E K Hussey, M J Clarke, A C Gilchrist, A Symonds, S K Warne, B Lee, S R Clark, G D McGrath

England: A J Strauss, A N Cook, I R Bell, P D Collingwood, A Flintoff, K P Pietersen, G O Jones, M S Panesar, M J Hoggard, S J Harmison, S I Mahmood

Australia won the toss and elected to bat

Thursday

14 December 2006

THIRD TEST, DAY ONE

As both teams arrived at the ground each of them were aware of the importance of this Test match. For England it was a 'must win' game and for Australia a win here would secure the return of that famous urn.

Perhaps the only Test match of the series where the toss was one you might prefer to lose, Andrew Flintoff did exactly that and was cordially invited by Ponting to take the field.

Looking focused as a unit, Freddie's men bowled well and, although conceding a flurry of runs in the first 45 minutes, chances could very easily have come their way.

Eventually it was left to the reliable Hoggard to tempt Hayden into a shot outside his off stump which, as the annoyance on his face showed, was to be his downfall as he nicked the ball through to Jones.

Harmison was then brought into the attack and, with his last chance to impress in this series, began to look a little more like the bowler of old. Bowling with decent pace and a controlled line both he and his partners at the other end restricted the Australians run rate to below three an over as they edged past fifty.

Perhaps stifled by the accuracy of the bowling Ponting, looking to drive a ball through mid-on, was then beaten by a Harmison delivery that straightened up on him a little and trapped him in front for just 2.

The wicket brought the in-form Hussey to the crease and through some tight and hostile bowling, the Australians edged their way towards the interval.

With just a few minutes left before the break, Flintoff turned to

PUTTING HIS HAND UP: Flintoff begins the England attack with the new ball

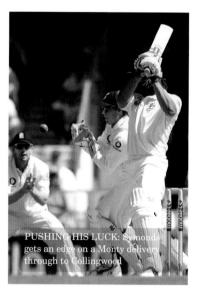

PUSHING HIS LUCK: Symonds gets an edge on a Monty delivery through to Collingwood

his new finger spinner Panesar to bowl a couple of overs. Beginning with a controlled maiden for his first over in Australia he was quickly to better that when, with the first delivery of his second, he got one to bounce and turn a little into the left-handed Langer and, with a look of almost disbelief passed between bat and pad to bowl him for 37 and bring the players in for an early lunch.

Now 69-3 England continued to apply pressure to the Australians with some aggressive and disciplined bowling. Hussey, at first looking a little edgy, moved his way into double figures while his partner Clarke appeared to be timing the ball with ease to bring up the Australian's ton.

With the score on 121 and with Harmison now looking something close to his best, the ever growing confidence of the bowler paid off as he beat Clarke for pace with a short ball the batsman chose to try and pull and succeeded only in sending back a return catch of the splice for 37.

That brought the latest recruit for the Australians to the middle

A GREAT DEBUT: Flintoff congratulates Monty on a great start to Test cricket down under

and Symonds, looking to be positive, decided to take on Panesar with some lusty blows out of the ground. Hitting an impressive 17 from just one Monty over, Flintoff, undaunted, kept faith in his spinner, a decision that was to prove correct, as Panesar, in the very next over, trapping Symonds for room and, assisted by the extra WACA bounce, had his man caught behind attempting to cut the ball through the off side.

Now 172-5 England were probably feeling justified in assuming they had taken the honours for the session so far and, if there was doubt in their minds, it was soon to be eradicated as the now boisterous crowd saw Panesar get another one to turn and bounce in to the new batsman Gilchrist for a fabulous bat-pad catch at short leg from Bell for a duck.

Hussey was now looking like the sole saviour for his team's innings and, with increased momentum, progressed his score past yet

another fifty and, with Warne, took the total past 200.

Warne, who had struck some of his customary blows on his way to a useful 25, now became Panesar's fourth wicket as, like Symonds, he edged an attempted cut into the hands of Jones behind the stumps.

Now seven down, Lee came to the crease and while Hussey was attempting to restrict the potency of Harmison at the other end Lee was doing his best to deal with Panesar in a mood for wickets.

Eventually it was to be Panesar who got his man and, with it, a fabulous 5-wicket haul on his debut in Australia. Trapping his man lbw for 10 he brought the Australian total to an incredible 234-8

Perhaps, with a certain air of justice, for an extremely good day's bowling from Harmison, it was he who quickly cleaned up the tail by first bowling Clark for 3 and then McGrath from a steepling short delivery to the alert hands of Cook at silly mid-off for 1.

With almost exactly one hour left before the end of play, England looked to play their normal game up until stumps.

Starting positively they quickly moved the score into the thirties, taking advantage of some very quick, but slightly wayward deliveries. However, about half way through the hour Cook, almost in expected fashion, was to find himself being drawn in, yet again, to a full delivery outside his off stump and edge the ball to Langer for 15.

Strauss, looking in good touch, was joined by Bell but, with only one further run added to the total, he too was to find himself heading back to the pavilion having got the slightest of nick on a fearsome Lee delivery.

Australia now sensed a turn around in their fortunes, and

bowling with tremendous pace, Lee, accompanied by McGrath, exerted huge pressure on the English batsmen.

With no further wicket over the next 15-20 minutes, Ponting made a double change to bring Warne and Clark into the attack.

Facing an extremely uncomfortable 10 minutes to the close both batsmen played Warne well but Collingwood could do nothing in his power to get his bat onto a Clark delivery. Playing and missing countless times he finally edged one through to Warne's left at first slip only for the veteran to put it down.

Grateful for his fortune, Collingwood and Strauss were both pleased and relieved to head back to the dressing room with their wickets still intact.

ALL TO PLAY FOR: Strauss and Collingwood leave the WACA for the first day

Brisbane

Adelaide

Perth

Melbourne

Sydney

Sydney

Melbourne

Perth

Adelaide

Brisbane

Thursday
14 December 2006

THIRD TEST, DAY ONE

After a day off and then two days of preparation we are ready to try and keep the series alive at Perth, but I woke up expecting not to play. Everyone knows how close Andrew Flintoff and I are, but even he didn't give anything away. Then the players were called together and he told us that Jimmy Anderson was being left out.

It was a relief because I felt I had improved at Adelaide, without the figures to back that up, and I knew there was better still to come.

We drummed into ourselves that we needed to seize the moment and any opportunities that came our way in Perth. If we could do that and stick to the plans we had stuck to so much of the time in Adelaide we felt we could win.

We were looking to bat first because it looked a decent surface

BACK TO HIS BEST: Harmison celebrates the important wicket of Ponting

but we lost the toss and then it came down to trying to take wickets early to apply a bit of pressure.

As always, Justin Langer and Matthew Hayden came hard at us early doors, but although they put on 47 in quick time, we felt we were putting the ball in decent areas.

Sure enough he went for another big drive off Hoggy and nicked it.

I had been a bit nervous again starting up and my plan was to bowl wide to Ponting and try to draw him across his stumps with a view to trapping him lbw with a straight one.

I wasn't bowling as full as I'd like, but the channel was right. Unfortunately, it wasn't doing a lot for my confidence because I wasn't making Ricky play. When I managed to push the ball in towards him that got him lbw it was an unbelievable moment for me. I had worked to a plan and dismissed the Australian captain. After all my troubles it was a huge lift and release of tension. Freddie came up to me about ten balls later and told me I was looking a totally different bowler. That's how much it meant to me.

We finished the first session on a real high because Monty got one past Langer and bowled him bang on the lunch interval. What I remember most about the moment was chasing after these two big hands and a turban trying to grab Monty and stop him running clean off the field and into the Barmy Army!

I had followed up by getting out Michael Clarke caught and bowled, taking the catch one-handed with my left hand and narrowly avoiding knocking the ball out again with my right hand as I swung around. I swear that if it had been the Western Australia match a few days earlier I would have done just that. Amazing what a difference a bit of confidence makes.

FLYING START: Monty jumps with joy in reaction to bowling Justin Langer

I enjoyed bowling to the tail on a pitch with bounce and managed to end the innings quickly by sending back Stuart Clark and Glenn McGrath. You try and put yourself in the batsman's shoes and work out what he is expecting. I would be expecting every ball around my head, so with a bit of double bluff I pitched one up and he missed it and was bowled. Glenn also missed it, but he was caught!

As we were walking off I said to Glenn "That's one all" because I didn't think I was out lbw to him in Adelaide. Australia were all out for 244. Happy days.

In the remaining play we lost Cook and Ian Bell in making 51, but still felt we were in the more promising position. It was Monty's day. He took 5-92 and stuck to his plan, even when coming under attack. Our plan is to build a sizeable lead on day two and put the Aussies on the back foot.

Thursday
14 December 2006

THIRD TEST, DAY ONE

On a WACA pitch more like we have come to expect in years gone by, it would be fair to say England have had the better of this first day. After Ricky won the toss and batted, experience told me we would have to play well for the first session.

Traditionally, batting is hard work for the first few hours of a WACA Test match and today was no exception. With a fair covering of patchy grass the ball carried beautifully through to the wicket-keeper and I am sure Messrs Harmison, Flintoff and Co would have been thrilled to see the ball rocketing through to Geraint Jones's gloves.

As we expected Monty Panesar was named in the England eleven at the expense of Ashley Giles, who I would suspect is feeling like the loneliest guy on the planet right now. He has been under the pump from all corners so it came as no surprise to see him omitted, even if it is a tough call on him.

Thanks to yours truly, Panesar had an instant impact on the game. With an over to go before lunch, the wily left-arm spinner snuck one past my pad and cleaned bowled me. To say I was surprised is an understatement as it was the first time in fifteen years of playing first-class cricket that I have been bowled by a spinner on the WACA.

In taking five wickets he has given England new hope for this series. Along with Steve Harmison, who is getting better with every outing to the crease, England today felt more like the team we played eighteen months ago. They bowled aggressively and fielded well and look to be up for this Test match. In many ways they have everything to gain from turning around their fortunes and today they showed great courage to get back into our faces.

Andrew Strauss came out blazing when it was England's turn to bat and it seems to us that England have planned to be much more aggressive than they have in the first two Tests. Whether this is a conscious plan I am not sure but I do know that for England to have any chance of getting back into this series, then a more positive approach is their best means.

With twelve wickets falling on the first day, the game is certainly going forward. Today was a day of high entertainment for yet another record-breaking crowd and I would imagine tomorrow will be just as intense. I wouldn't be at all surprised to see this wicket even tougher to bat on tomorrow as it gets a little quicker than it was today. Whatever way, when there is pace and bounce in the surface, everyone accepts the batsmen will leave the ground with a smile on their faces because there is nothing like seeing great fast bowling, wily spinners and a few odd boundaries like we witnessed today.

HEAD DOWN: Justin looks to see off the new ball

Brisbane
Adelaide
Perth
Melbourne
Sydney

View from the Boundary

Friday
15 December 2006

THIRD TEST, DAY TWO

England began the day with high hopes of converting their first-innings bowling performance into a match-winning effort but, within minutes of the resumption of play, their plans were to be readjusted by the opposition.

Having played with little certainty the night before Collingwood again looked edgy in the middle and, soon after tentatively pushing at a few deliveries, drove with little commitment at a short of a length ball from McGrath only to watch it fly off a thick edge into the hands of Hayden at gully for 11.

That brought Pietersen to the middle and with it, a sense that if England could push the score forward quickly, in a low-scoring game such as this, a positive result was very much still on the cards.

Both players looked fluent at the crease and added another 30 to the total before Strauss on 42 and looking to post his first significant effort of the series, was adjudged to have edged a Clark delivery to Gilchrist. It was a decision that dismayed the batsman and, as subsequent TV evidence showed, Strauss appeared to have just cause for disappointment.

Flintoff, now at the middle, appeared to be showing real signs of his lack of match practice as he attempted, in vain, to push the scoring on. Eventually, with just 13 to his name, he was to fall victim to Symonds with a loose shot outside

SOLITARY RESISTANCE: Pietersen, once again, leads from the front on his way to a belligerent 70

off stump that edged a low chance to the grateful Warne.

Now 107-5 England were on the brink of throwing away their previous day's advantage.

Pietersen, looking as commanding as ever, attempted to maintain a level of authority about the England innings but, just 7 runs later his partner Jones, in an effort to push the scoring on, drove at a Symonds half volley, only to edge it to the ever-safe hands of Hayden at gully for 0.

Now England were in trouble with their tail exposed and while Pietersen attempted to rotate the strike as sensibly as he could Mamood, perhaps inspired by his partner's heroics, was to fall victim to an over ambitious hook stroke that succeeded only in top edging the ball through to the keeper.

Pietersen, now with the more resolute Hoggard, did his best to protect the strike from his partner

FIRST BLOOD: Collingwood falls to McGrath early on in the day

out the best fielder in the Australian side for a fabulous 70.

Now, it appeared, would be the last couple of deliveries of the innings but Panesar and Harmison were to have other ideas. With a combination of clever singles and some uncharacteristically orthodox stroke play, both batsmen frustrated the Australians with a innings-best partnership of 40 before Harmison, on a very credible 23, finally succumbed to a attempted pull through mid-wicket which he top edged to Clarke at mid-on to end the England innings.

With a small lead of 29 Australia came to the middle with high hopes of putting themselves in a dominant position by the close of play. However, with the first ball of their innings Hoggard beat Langer with a late in-swinger that went between bat and pad to bowl the opener for 0.

Buoyed by the early wicket, England felt they were in with a chance to get on top of the Australians but, with a combination of fine orthodox batting and a pitch that appeared to be playing better with each passing hour, both batsmen progressed chancelessly to their fifties and closed the day out on a lead of 148.

while doing his utmost to move the total forward as quickly as possible. Ponting, instructing six of his available fielders to the boundary for each Pietersen delivery, did his best to contain him but, with customary flamboyance and arrogance Kevin moved to another fifty.

Finally Hoggard faced one ball too many and Warne, beating him with added bounce and turn had Matthew edging a simple chance to Hayden at slip for 4.

Now Pietersen, accompanied by Harmison, had no choice but to attack and, over the next 20 minutes or so, entertained a capacity crowd with a range of extraordinary shots to all parts of the ground. Doing his best to keep strike and be ruthlessly attacking at all times, eventually saw his demise as, in an attempt to pull a quick delivery from Lee well outside his off stump, he managed only to get underneath it and pick

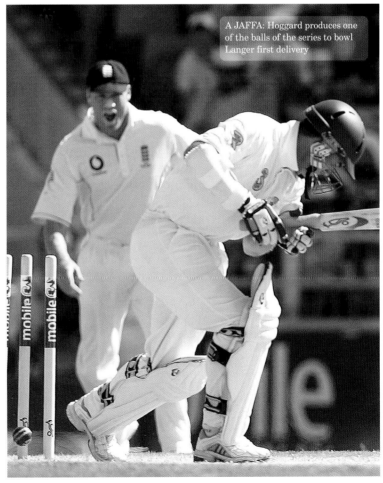

A JAFFA: Hoggard produces one of the balls of the series to bowl Langer first delivery

Friday
15 December 2006

THIRD TEST, DAY TWO

Although we lost Paul Collingwood early, we felt we were really starting to get going when Andrew Strauss and Kevin Pietersen took the score to 82-3. Then Straussy got another poor decision and, before we knew it, we were 155-8 and the tail had the job of trying to get as close to Australia's score as possible.

All we needed to do was bat with KP because he was in such unbelievable form.

The disappointing thing about our batting was that when they got on top we didn't see the good spell off as Hussey had done making 74 not out on day one. We tended to get frustrated and go at a ball when we thought it was there to be hit. Clark bowls in good areas and just tries to dry the batsmen up so they take risks. He is the perfect foil for Shane Warne at the other end because Australia can attack with Warne, knowing the game is not going to be taken away from them

with someone as accurate as Clark operating in tandem.

By the time I went in at number ten we were still 89 runs behind and just had to whittle away at that deficit. I managed to add 20 with Kev before he was out for 70 and then it was down to Monty and me to see if we could at least end the innings on a high note.

I wasn't sure how to play when Monty came in. Brett Lee was bowling quickly from one end and Warney was being Warney from the other end. I'd been in for six or seven overs and was seeing the ball well so my first thought was to try and protect Monty a bit without going over the top. The last thing we wanted was him breaking a finger facing Lee.

I've managed to keep the strike for a couple of overs and then Monty has found himself facing Clark, who bowled him a straight one which he's hit back past him with a shot Brian Lara would have been proud of. I thought 'F*** me, and I've been trying to protect this guy!' From then on I let him get on with it and we had some good fun putting on 40 and gaining England some momentum again at the end of a disappointing innings.

We've come out thinking we're on a bit of a roll and Matthew Hoggard knocks over Langer first ball with a beauty. Australia are effectively 29-1 and it's game on. But the wicket had slowed up and gone flat.

The best time to bat was probably day two and the first half of day three. We had wasted the opportunity to use the pitch at its best. Hayden and Ponting cashed in, playing well for the rest of the day. We tried bowling short at them and used Monty over and around the wicket, but credit where credit's due. Matthew and Ricky played very well.

LOOKING IN GOOD TOUCH: Strauss pulls one through mid-wicket

Friday

15 December 2006

THIRD TEST, DAY TWO

If England had the better of us yesterday then we certainly turned things around today. In the context of the series today could turn out to be one of the most significant.

Arriving at the ground, England had an opportunity to take this game away from us but thanks to a brilliant performance from all of our bowlers, we stole back the momentum and go into day three as red-hot favourites for this match.

Before the game I mentioned the impact Andrew Symonds could potentially have on this game and although he only scored 25 runs with the bat he saved about that amount of runs in the field and also took two vital wickets, bowling his medium pacers. Players are usually judged on statistics in this game but people like Symmo have an X factor which makes him such a valuable member of the team. His personality within the group is infectious, as is his aura, so statistics alone can never tell the true value of his presence in the baggy green cap.

With Ricky and Matty Hayden at the crease and a forecast temperature of 36 degrees tomorrow we know we are now in the box seat to grind England out of this game. Test cricket has a funny way of changing from hour to hour, day to day, but we are starting to taste the addictive tastes of victory. Experience tells us our main enemy is getting too far ahead of ourselves before the job is done, but the disappointment of our last Ashes campaign is sure to keep us focused for at least another two days.

ALL SMILES: Symonds grabs the important wicket of Flintoff

Brisbane

Adelaide

Perth

Melbourne

Sydney

View from the Boundary

Saturday

16 December 2006

THIRD TEST, DAY THREE

England began the day with, perhaps, their last chance of saving this Test match and with it, the Ashes.

Australia, with an overnight lead of 148, looked to dominate early on and, despite some promising bowling, hit a quick 25 runs in the opening 15 minutes. Harmison, bowling now at something like his best, was getting the ball to swing away from the right handers and, deservedly so, drew Ponting into a drive outside his off stump to a delivery that just straightened a little and caught the edge through to Jones for a well-made 75.

Hoggard now on at the other end, replacing the off spin of Pietersen, was also bowling with excellent accuracy and a small amount of swing and, between them, the England pair began to

NO ANSWER: England bowl with little luck as the runs begin to pile up

exert some pressure on the top order batsmen.

Just two overs later Harmison, the ball swinging in late to the left-handed Hayden, had a very positive appeal for leg before turned down by the umpire and a little of the pressure was released for the Australians.

As Harmison ended his good spell, which had seen a number of appeals and an edge drop short of slip, it was time for the ever exuberant Panesar to see if he could get something out of this game. Almost immediately he looked aggressive and, he too, was unlucky to have a bad-pad chance turned down by the umpires from the enormously dangerous Michael Hussey.

As Hayden neared his century though, Panesar was to get some reward for his efforts as, in an attempt to cut a shortish delivery from Monty through backward point, a little extra bounce resulted in the ball catching the top edge of Hayden's bat for a lightning-fast catch to Collingwood at slip. Reacting quickly, Collingwood, in the pose of a goalkeeper tipping one over the bar, managed to parry the ball up into the air for an excellent deflected catch.

Australia, now 235 ahead, were three down as they neared the interval and, with some resolute batting from Hussey and Clarke managed to see themselves into the lunch break despite continuing pressure from the England bowlers.

The next session, unlike the morning, was to be almost without chance as the Australians began to take the game away from the English. Playing positively when possible and taking advantage of the flattening WACA wicket, both batsmen progressed the score with relative ease as the English fielders toiled in 38-degree temperatures.

With Hussey nearing yet another century, he offered a sharp chance to Strauss standing at a very wide first slip but, with that not taken, he progressed to three figures and, with it, brought his Test-match average up to an incredible 90 runs.

Clarke too, looked in complete control as both batsmen completed a wicket-less session into tea.

Finally, just after the break, the deadlock was broken as Panesar got his reward for a good spell of bowling with the wicket of Hussey caught behind by Jones.

Now with an enormous 357-4 on the board, England had been pretty much batted out of this game as Symonds came to the wicket, but their hopes were temporarily

SOME RARE DELIGHT: Collingwood pulls off an athletic catch to dismiss Hayden

succession of bowlers in an attempt to restrict the unstoppable flow of runs from the wicket-keeper's bat.

Soon, with no bowler finding an answer to his stroke-play, Gilchrist was nearing in on the 21- year-old record held by the great Viv Richards for the fastest Test match century in history. With a 56-ball ton to beat, Gilly missed out by just 2 deliveries as he moved to one of the most exciting Test-match hundreds of all time.

While the crowd were still celebrating his achievement, Ponting decided enough was enough and brought his men in to leave the English facing an enormous total and an awkward 20 minutes to the close.

England, with a massive 557 needed to win, had the worst possible start as Lee, in the first over of the England innings got a ball to swing back into the left-handed Strauss.

Andrew, perhaps misjudging the line, fatefully left the ball and, although TV replays showed he might again have been unlucky with the umpire's decision, he found himself heading back to the pavilion for a duck.

Cook, now joined by Bell, looked focused and surprisingly at ease, given the situation, as they took England to the close without further loss.

LICENSE TO THRILL: Gilchrist, with a huge total behind him, throws caution to the wind

restored when he too was quickly dismissed by Panesar, caught in the slips by Collingwood for just 2.

At 365-5 England were perhaps hopeful that they could restrict the opposition to a lead of around 450 but, in the following minutes that dream was to be shattered as Gilchrist, given licence to attack by his team's predicament, needed no second invitation.

Whilst Clarke moved fluently to record his second Test century in consecutive games the crowd could have been forgiven for not noticing as Gilchrist, timing the ball with unequalled ease, quickly raced to fifty with a flurry of boundaries.

Hitting an incredible 24 from one Panesar over, Flintoff turned to a

Brisbane

Adelaide

Perth

Melbourne

Sydney

Sydney

Melbourne

Perth

Adelaide

Brisbane

Saturday
16 December 2006

THIRD TEST, DAY THREE

Did I say we had found a way to bowl to Adam Gilchrist? The day started well for us when I got Ricky Ponting to nick one and dismissed him for the second time in the match with Australia 173 ahead.

We were happy enough at that point because we were bowling in some good areas and had a new batsman in Hussey to bowl at. I had an lbw shout against Hayden which I thought was stone dead, but wasn't given, and then Hussey nicked one just short of slip before hooking one that has dropped between three England players, including Geraint Jones.

Australia could have been 150-4 instead of 150-2 and those are sometimes the fine lines between success and failure. If Gilchrist had come in on a pair with his side in a bit of trouble his state of mind would have been a lot different to when he did actually appear, by which time Australia were 365-5.

He could so easily have been out early as he played a ball in the air just out of reach of second gully, but suddenly he was off the pair and 50-odd balls later he had got a hundred.

We had nine men on the boundary at one stage and he was hitting the ball over the top of all of us. When someone of his ability plays like that there isn't much you can do. I came off at tea happy enough with my efforts and with figures of 1-50 off 16 overs. I felt I had turned the corner and things were starting to go for me. By the end of the day I had 1-116 from 24 overs, having seen the ball disappear to all parts. No matter

A DIFFERENT BOWLER FROM BRISBANE: Harmy gets the wicket on Ponting for the second time in the match

where you pitched the ball Gilly went for it. Did I have a plan? I think the only one that occurred to me was to try and bowl under-arm so he could get the bat underneath the ball!

I bowled a good length around the wicket and he's got a thick edge wide of third-man for four. I pitched it fuller and he's managed to get his hands free and drag it over mid-wicket for four. I tried a short one and he's hit me between fine leg and backward square for four. He was in one of those destructive modes he can adopt

when he gets in and he has taken the game away from us totally.

Australia have declared on 527-5, leaving us a massive 557 to win and still more than two days to play, making a draw the least likely result. We had to bat for six and a bit sessions and if we did we would win. It was a massively tall order, even before Andrew Strauss got another iffy decision to be out for a duck as we made 19-1 before the close. We were left clutching at straws again, but looked at it that we would need to build partnerships on day four.

Saturday
16 December 2006

THIRD TEST, DAY THREE

I hardly know where to start after today's demolition job at the WACA. Yesterday showed great fighting spirit from the Australian cricket team, today was simple carnage.

Three centuries, a ninety and a 75 from the captain set up an incredible platform for us to take back the Ashes within the next forty-eight hours.

So classy was Adam Gilchrist's rapid-fire century that the other stars of today almost went forgotten. Michael Hussey and Michael Clarke were brilliant, as was Matthew Hayden, who showed

MR CRICKET: Hussey brings up yet another big score as his Test average nears 90

A CLASS ACT: Gilchrist celebrates his rapid-fire century

once again why he is arguably the greatest opening batsman of the modern era.

England had few answers after the first hour and we were surprised when they opened the bowling with Kevin Pietersen with a relatively new ball. Giving guys like Matthew and Ricky even a few sighters at the start of the day is an interesting tactic which we suspect England might take back if they had another chance at it.

While it is always easy with the benefit of hindsight we were also interested in the lack of overs bowled by Mahmood throughout this second innings. As a new bowler to the team, we thought Andrew Flintoff might have shown a little more faith in him but I guess when our batsmen were going like they were it is the more experienced players whom the captain generally calls upon.

In our changing room the main discussion was whether to declare before stumps or to keep batting on. The consensus was split but after the tidal wave of momentum

ignited by Gilly, we thought it might be worth a few overs at England's openers. Thankfully for us the decision paid dividends with the dismissal of England's most stubborn runmaker in Andrew Strauss. His loss tonight is huge for us and a further nightmare for the visitors. As I mentioned during the last Test there is nothing worse for an opening batsman than having to bat just before stumps and I felt a bit sorry for Straussy when he was given out lbw in the first over.

Having said that and with the Ashes up for grabs, maybe I didn't feel that sorry for my good mate from Middlesex. It was just great to see the back of him after what was an amazing day from our eyes. The feeling in our changing rooms is cock-a-hoop and while we know we still have to take nine wickets in very hot conditions tomorrow we are getting closer and closer every day to reclaiming the Ashes.

The excitement is almost too much to bear but the hard work from now on in will be worth every single ounce of effort.

SETTLING IN FOR A LONG DAY: Bell and Cook contemplate the long task ahead of them

Sunday

17 December 2006

THIRD TEST, DAY FOUR

It is on days like these that you are reminded of the truly unique nature of Test-match cricket. In a game where, for the most part, there are long periods without significant incident, the play remains utterly enthralling throughout.

England, resuming on 19-1, began, with great purpose, the gargantuan task of batting out 12 sessions if they were to grab a draw or even, perhaps, a miraculous victory.

Bell and Cook both played with enormous concentration and determination and, assisted by a pitch that was flattening out, managed to see their team through, without incident to the lunch break and, with it, compile over 100 runs.

Both players soon reached their fifties and, with the Australians beginning to look a little weary in the 30-degree temperatures, continued to build an impressive partnership.

Eventually, after a fantastic stand of 170 Bell was to drive at a ball outside his off stump from Warne that he didn't quite get to the pitch of and, instead, with great dismay, he firmly drove the ball into the hands of Langer at short cover.

Disappointed as they were, England must have been satisfied to have lasted some 3 ½ hours before the loss of their first wicket and, with Collingwood coming to the middle, a sense of optimism washed over the ground as the thought of the unlikeliest of draws seemed a faint possibility.

However, that optimism was soon to be given a reality check as, just

RESISTANCE BROKEN: Bell drives a Warne delivery into the hands of Langer at short cover

15 runs later, Collingwood got the thinnest of edges from a Clark delivery through to Gilchrist for just 5.

Now 185-3 Cook nearing his century was joined by Pietersen. The Australians, knowing that while he remains at the crease any result is possible, did their best to remove him but, with typical aggression, Kevin moved quickly into double figures.

Finally, after nearly five hours at the crease and under the most intense pressure, Cook managed to grab the single he needed to bring

up his finest, and probably most significant, century of his blossoming career.

He and Pietersen then continued to build a solid partnership that took them to within just 17 deliveries of the close of play before, devastatingly for the tourists, Glen McGrath managed to temp Cook to push at one outside his off stump, and he and the huge English fan base at the WACA watched with anguish as it sailed into the safe gloves of Gilchrist.

Having got so far it was a bitter-sweet moment for the young player

as, in the enjoyment of his achievement, he was visibly distraught at the timing of his dismissal.

With such a short amount of time remaining before the close England opted to send Matthew Hoggard into the middle to see off the remaining deliveries. However, their plan was to be undone as McGrath was not finished yet and, just two balls later, got one straight through the Yorkshireman to bowl him for 0.

Flintoff now, not wishing to send any others in his place, nervously saw himself and the team through to the close and to a situation that they would, perhaps, have settled for at the beginning of play but one, given the timing of their mini collapse, might have helped swing the momentum of the game away from them.

LAST STAND: Flintoff and Pietersen leave the field of play with still a day's batting to survive

View from the Boundary

FRIENDLY BANTER: The Aussie fans cheer and jeer in the hot Perth sunshine

Steve Harmison

Sunday
17 December 2006

THIRD TEST, DAY FOUR

Again the day started well for us with Alastair Cook and Ian Bell batting well and carrying out our plan by taking their second-wicket partnership to 170.

Thinking back, if Gilchrist had been caught at gully for nought the night before we could so easily be still in with a winning chance. Even chasing 500-odd at 170-1 you are starting to think what might be possible if we could only go through this day losing no more than three wickets.

For so long that looked like being the case. At 21, Cook has so much talent and so much to offer the

England team in years to come. His fourth Test century was a triumph for patience and sticking it out when the bowlers were on top. At the end of the day his wicket, followed closely by that of nightwatchman Matthew Hoggard, has all but extinguished our last glimmer of hope. But for Alastair to come off bitterly disappointed at getting out for 116 in an Ashes Test against Australia says everything about him.

He was shattered at not seeing the day out, but he had played magnificently. He's a great team man and a bright lad, who will argue that black is white when he's in the mood. I would describe Cooky as a young man with an older man's head on his shoulders. I've spent a fair bit of time with him since he came to India with us and he's someone I think an awful lot of. He is so mature for 21 and I

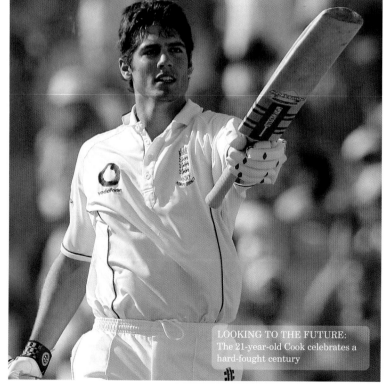

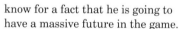
LOOKING TO THE FUTURE:
The 21-year-old Cook celebrates a
hard-fought century

know for a fact that he is going to have a massive future in the game.

Australia bowled really well at him and dried him up for periods, but when that happened he just got behind the ball and waited for his chance to score. Ian Bell adopted a similar approach in a terrific partnership. Paul Collingwood fell cheaply, but KP was again in good touch to be 37 not out at the end of the day and who knows what might have happened if Cooky had managed to survive those last few overs. We might have closed on 270-3 and, with a good start on day five, given the Aussies something to think about. As it was Glenn McGrath found an edge and the plan to send Hoggy in to protect Freddie Flintoff's wicket backfired when Glenn bowled him with a great Yorker. At 265-5 we knew it was going to take something very special to keep the series alive.

KEEPING FOCUS: Bell plays watchfully through the opening session

England looked to be well and truly on the ropes and we hoped for a quick reclaiming of the little urn. Unfortunately England had a different plan and as it stands the game is still well and truly on.

Admittedly the wickets of Cook and Hoggard in the last few overs have given us a reasonably firm hold on the match but with Kevin Pietersen at the wicket and in outstanding form and Andrew Flintoff due to score some runs, England will still rate themselves a chance of taking out a miracle victory. The way these last two series have been played we have all come to expect the unexpected so until the final wicket is taken or the final run scored then no one will be taking anything for granted.

Regardless of the result tomorrow England are sure to take great confidence out of the innings of Ian Bell and Alastair Cook. Both of these young players batted very well in the face of the most pressure they are ever likely to face in Test cricket.

With an Ashes series on the line, and facing the likes of Warne, McGrath, Lee and Clark, they should both be very proud of the way they played today. From my eyes today was nearly as tough as it gets and they both passed the test very well.

For us we hung in there all day on a flattening WACA surface. The rewards for our persistent hard work might have come late in the day but we know we are that little bit closer again to winning this series tomorrow. England will need to be brilliant, we just need to be as tight as we were today and the urn will be back in Australia by tomorrow night.

Sunday
17 December 2006

THIRD TEST, DAY FOUR

The most interesting thing about today was that although we spent ninety overs in the field, the time seemed to pass like the blink of an eye. I guess there was so much to play for and we became so involved in the contest, we didn't have time to look up at the clock or worry about how tiring today actually was.

Now as I sit here on my computer I realise that the heat and the pressure of the battle has taken its toll because my feet, legs and back are aching and my eyes are stinging and very, very sleepy.

When we arrived this morning we could have been forgiven for getting a bit far ahead of ourselves.

IMPORTANT WICKET: Clark celebrates the removal of the dogged Collingwood for just 5

Brisbane

Adelaide

Perth

Melbourne

Sydney

View from the Boundary

Monday

18 December 2006

THIRD TEST, DAY FIVE

England, having lost two wickets late in the day yesterday, knew that they were really up against it if they were to save the Ashes.

Flintoff, who has struggled for form with the bat so far in this series, began nervously but then, almost without warning, took on the Australian bowlers in a brief 5-6 over spell hitting 30 runs in half as many deliveries and, for a moment, sewing the seed of optimism amongst his team-mates.

However, unfortunately for the visiting side, his burst was relatively short-lived and, having brought up an entertaining fifty, he was deceived by the drift and flight of a Warne delivery to end his innings on 51.

The Australians, now with that crucial first wicket of the day behind them, began to sense the opportunity to wrap up the series and, not long after, Warne, whilst appealing for a leg-before decision against Jones, was left almost as bemused as the batsman as Ponting, noticing that he was just out of his ground, swooped in from silly mid-off, picked up the ball and threw down the stumps to complete a miserable Test match for the wicket-keeper/batsman.

Now seven down and with Mahmood in the middle the Aussies began to taste the victory they had worked so hard for. Pietersen, leaving his partner to face his fair share of the deliveries was, perhaps, ruing his decision as, just nine runs into their brief partnership, Mahmood was caught in front of his stumps to a Yorker-length delivery and given out lbw for 4.

Eight down, Harmison came to the centre looking to help his team through the final 10 minutes before lunch but, very first delivery, attempted to sweep Warne off a full-length ball and he too found himself being faced by the umpire's finger for 0.

England managed to see off the last few deliveries before lunch but went into the changing room nine down and almost inevitable defeat.

ONE TO GO: Warne traps Harmison lbw for 0

Sure enough, just moments after the resumption, Monty Panesar, who had until this point, achieved a fabulous debut in Australia, was to face the master of his craft in a mood to finish things off and, like 698 Test victims before him, Monty became Warne's penultimate scalp in his pursuit of a staggering 700 Test wickets.

Australia, with obvious delight and jubilation had completed a 206-run victory and, with it, successfully regained the legendary little urn with an unassailable 3-0 lead in the series.

TEAM EFFORT: The Australian side proudly pose with the urn

Brisbane
Adelaide
Perth
Melbourne
Sydney

View from the Boundary

DONE IT: The players leap in delight as Warne bowls Panesar to win back the Ashes

Brisbane

Adelaide

Perth

Melbourne

Sydney

Steve Harmison

Monday
18 December 2006

THIRD TEST, DAY FIVE

Kevin Pietersen and Freddie were together at the start of the day and for us to win both had to score 150. They've both got that in them, but it was clearly an unlikely scenario. Fred had looked in good form with the bat at times earlier in the series without getting a score and here he clearly decided attack was the best policy.

He started to hit the ball well again and, even if we weren't going to win, I felt that this was going to be the innings that really brought him back to top form and set him up for the rest of the series. He got to 51 and had put on 75 with KP when Warney got him with an absolute beauty that dipped late

SOLE SURVIVOR: Pietersen once again finds himself with the tail

and crept under his bat to bowl him. It's a method of dismissal Shane has successfully employed many times in his amazing career and it signalled the beginning of the end for us.

All hope had gone and that being the case the last four wickets fell quickly. Geraint's was a strange one and summed up his tour. He didn't know where the ball had gone as he went to sweep and thought his back foot was in his crease. He was bitterly disappointed and things have gone against him on this trip, but I know he has what it takes to bounce back. Warney did me first ball lbw, which was how he did me on a number of occasions during the last Ashes series. I had formulated a plan to counteract that and it seemed to be working up to this innings. I thought the ball had pitched outside leg stump and went to sweep. By that time the party atmosphere was already starting in the ground because it was clear Australia had won back the Ashes.

When the game was over and we got back to the dressing room we were downbeat, upset, disappointed, all the emotions you would expect. We had to watch as the Australians celebrated. It wasn't easy, but we had no complaints because we had been just as mad in our celebrations two years ago.

They deserve the Ashes. They were the better team over the three Test matches so far and it was a role reversal of two years earlier because all their big players found their form at the right time, while some of ours struggled. Bad as we were feeling, we knew that is what makes it so special when you win. It was devastating watching those celebrations, but I'm sure the likes of Ponting, Hayden and Langer were feeling just as devastated two years ago and they have proved you can bounce back from setbacks.

We have to take it on the chin and we have to learn from the experience. About nine of our players just sat in the dressing room for hours after the game chewing the fat over where we had gone wrong and what we could have done better. I think Andrew Strauss hit the nail on the head when he said Australia would have been asking the same questions of themselves after the last series.

We had a beer and tried to get each other's spirits up because we don't want to lose the series 5-0. At the end of the day the Ashes were gone and we had to regroup.

ASHES *frontline*

Monday

18 December 2006

THIRD TEST, DAY FIVE

There is an historic moment in Australian sport when Cathy Freeman, the world 400-metre champion, finished her gold medal run in the Olympic final. With the weight of expectation resting heavily on her shoulders, she crossed the finishing line and then crouched down onto her knees with the most extraordinary expression painted across her face.

Her initial emotion didn't seem to be of jubilation or exhilaration but rather of sheer relief. She just sat on the track like a little school girl relieved at having passed the ultimate test. Yesterday, I could identify with her reaction. When Shane Warne bowled Monty Panesar with another perfect leg spinner my initial response was to jump around and dance and sing and rejoice to the tune of a successful Ashes campaign. But, after a couple of seconds all I really wanted to do was sit down in the middle of the WACA and reflect on what had just occurred. Physically I was tired, mentally I was exhausted and all I wanted to do was simply crouch down and take it all in.

The Australian sections of the crowd were going berserk, my team-mates were running to all corners to soak up the adulation, the cameras were rolling and looking for a few spontaneous quotes and the spirit of cricket was drifting gleefully through the air around the WACA.

In our changing room the mood was a mixture of raw emotion and genuine reflection. Most of the younger generation were taking in the party atmosphere, while some of the older crew, or 'dad's army' as we have been recently described, sat back like proud and fulfilled Indian chiefs pondering the future and enjoying the fruits of a job very well done.

Once again we had to come back from behind in this Test. After the first day and having been bowled out for 244, England should have been right in the box seat. We knew we were under the pump after a poor first-innings showing but thanks to another outstanding team performance in the field, we were able to claw the game back to our advantage.

When our turn came to bat again, the game was still well and truly up for grabs, but thanks to a remarkable performance from Matty Hayden, Ricky, Michael Clarke, Michael Hussey and Adam Gilchrist we were able put the match out of England's reach.

Gilly's innings was so devastating that the brilliant innings of the others almost paled into insignificance. At the end of our vice-captain's onslaught Haydos turned to me and said 'did that actually just happen? I can't believe what I have just seen.'

Imagine, if his team-mates couldn't believe it, how England must have felt? Here they are scrapping their way back into a Test series only to be demoralised by one of the most lethal players the world has ever seen.

From that moment when Gilly went passed 100, we knew the game would be ours if we were willing to put in another day or so of really hard work. And, to the credit of all of my team-mates, we fought and fought against a stubborn England outfit to finally come out triumphant, four and a half sessions of cricket later.

The obvious question is how do I feel right now? Well, the answer to that is, that besides being a little hung over, I feel incredibly satisfied and fulfilled. I have thought about this moment since 12 September last year.

We have worked hard, prepared meticulously and urged each other through boot camps and other Test series so that we would be ready to reclaim the Ashes from England. Now the job is done I feel absolutely thrilled and in a few days time I will start preparing for round four in front of 100,000 people at the MCG.

It just doesn't get much better than that.

SHOWING HIS COLOURS: Langer grabs an Aussie flag as celebrations begin

Scorecard

Australia 1st Innings

			Runs	Balls	4s	6s
J L Langer		b M S Panesar	37	68	6	0
M L Hayden	c G O Jones	b M J Hoggard	24	33	3	0
R T Ponting	lbw	b S J Harmison	2	11	0	0
M E K Hussey	not out		74	161	10	0
M J Clarke	c and b	b S J Harmison	37	67	4	0
A Symonds	c G O Jones	b M S Panesar	26	30	2	2
A C Gilchrist	c I R Bell	b M S Panesar	0	4	0	0
S K Warne	c G O Jones	b M S Panesar	25	23	3	0
B Lee	lbw	b M S Panesar	10	25	2	0
S R Clark		b S J Harmison	3	5	0	0
G D McGrath	c A N Cook	b S J Harmison	1	2	0	0
Extras		4nb 1w	5			
Total		all out	**244**	(71.0 ovs)		

Bowling	O	M	R	W
M J Hoggard	12	2	40	1
A Flintoff	9	2	36	0
S J Harmison	19	4	48	4
M S Panesar	24	4	92	5
S I Mahmood	7	2	28	0

Fall of wicket

47 (M L Hayden), 54 (R T Ponting), 69 (J L Langer), 121 (M J Clarke), 172 (A Symonds), 172 (A C Gilchrist), 214 (S K Warne), 234 (B Lee), 242 (S R Clark), 244 (G D McGrath)

England 1st Innings

			Runs	Balls	4s	6s
A J Strauss	c A C Gilchrist	b S R Clark	42	71	6	0
A N Cook	c J L Langer	b G D McGrath	15	15	2	0
I R Bell	c A C Gilchrist	b B Lee	0	2	0	0
P D Collingwood	c M L Hayden	b G D McGrath	11	33	1	0
K P Pietersen	c A Symonds	b B Lee	70	123	8	1
A Flintoff	c S K Warne	b A Symonds	13	31	2	0
G O Jones	c J L Langer	b A Symonds	0	4	0	0
S I Mahmood	c A C Gilchrist	b S R Clark	10	18	1	0
M J Hoggard	c M L Hayden	b S K Warne	4	39	0	0
S J Harmison	c B Lee	b S R Clark	23	33	3	0
M S Panesar	not out		16	26	3	0
Extras		10nb 1w	11			
Total		all out	**215**	(64.1 ovs)		

Bowling	O	M	R	W
B Lee	18	1	69	2
G D McGrath	18	5	48	2
S R Clark	15.1	3	49	3
S K Warne	9	0	41	1
A Symonds	4	1	8	2

Fall of wicket

36 (A N Cook), 37 (I R Bell), 55 (P D Collingwood), 82 (A J Strauss), 107 (A Flintoff), 114 (G O Jones), 128 (S I Mahmood), 155 (M J Hoggard), 175 (K P Pietersen), 215 (S J Harmison)

ASHES *frontline*

Australia 2nd Innings

			Runs	Balls	4s	6s
J L Langer		b M J Hoggard	0	1	0	0
M L Hayden	c P D Collingwood	b M S Panesar	92	159	12	0
R T Ponting	c G O Jones	b S J Harmison	75	128	10	0
M E K Hussey	c G O Jones	b M S Panesar	103	156	12	0
M J Clarke	not out		135	164	17	1
A Symonds	c P D Collingwood	b M S Panesar	2	6	0	0
A C Gilchrist	not out		102	59	12	4
Extras		1nb 2w 15lb	18			
Total		for 5	**527**	(112.0 ovs)		

Bowling	O	M	R	W
M J Hoggard	20	4	85	1
A Flintoff	19	2	76	0
S J Harmison	24	3	116	1
M S Panesar	34	3	145	3
S I Mahmood	10	0	59	0
K P Pietersen	5	1	31	0

Fall of wicket

0 (J L Langer), 144 (R T Ponting), 206 (M L Hayden), 357 (M E K Hussey), 365 (A Symonds)

England 2nd Innings

			Runs	Balls	4s	6s
A J Strauss	lbw	b B Lee	0	4	0	0
A N Cook	c A C Gilchrist	b G D McGrath	116	290	9	0
I R Bell	c J L Langer	b S K Warne	87	163	8	2
P D Collingwood	c A C Gilchrist	b S R Clark	5	36	0	0
K P Pietersen	not out		60	150	6	0
M J Hoggard		b G D McGrath	0	2	0	0
A Flintoff		b S K Warne	51	67	8	1
G O Jones	run out		0	7	0	0
S I Mahmood	lbw	b S R Clark	4	10	0	0
S J Harmison	lbw	b S K Warne	0	1	0	0
M S Panesar		b S K Warne	1	9	0	0
Extras		5nb 6w 11b 4lb	26			
Total		all out	**350**	(122.2 ovs)		

Bowling	O	M	R	W
B Lee	22	3	75	1
G D McGrath	27	9	61	2
S R Clark	25	7	56	2
S K Warne	39.2	6	115	4
A Symonds	9	1	28	0

Fall of wicket

0 (A J Strauss), 170 (I R Bell), 185 (P D Collingwood), 261 (A N Cook), 261 (M J Hoggard), 336 (A Flintoff), 336 (G O Jones), 345 (S I Mahmood), 346 (S J Harmison), 350 (M S Panesar)

Australia **beat England by 206 runs**

Brisbane
Adelaide
Perth
Melbourne
Sydney

FOURTH TEST
Melbourne
Melbourne Cricket Ground

View from the Boundary

Sydney

Melbourne

Perth

Adelaide

Brisbane

Teams

Umpires: Aleem Dar, R E Koertzen

Australia: J L Langer, M L Hayden, R T Ponting, M E K Hussey, M J Clarke, A Symonds, A C Gilchrist, S K Warne, B Lee, S R Clark, G D McGrath

England: A J Strauss, A N Cook, I R Bell, P D Collingwood, K P Pietersen, A Flintoff, C M W Read, S I Mahmood, M J Hoggard, S J Harmison, M S Panesar

England won the toss and elected to bat

Tuesday
26 December 2006

FOURTH TEST, DAY ONE

The MCG is always a special occasion on any Boxing Day and the first day of the fourth Test in this series was no exception.

With Warne on the brink of a remarkable 700 Test wickets, the Melbourne crowd filled the ground in anticipation of a fantastic day's play.

The 90,000-strong home crowd, perhaps relieved to lose the toss in difficult weather conditions, saw Andrew Flintoff elect to bat. With intermittent rain and a pitch showing response to the seamers, it was soon to be a decision that Freddie was to question.

Following on from his innings at the WACA, Cook appeared more confident in his footwork against an opening spell of bowling that contained a collection of troublesome deliveries.

However, only 23 runs into the innings, Cook, caught in two minds as to how to deal with a pacey Lee delivery, half got his bat out of the way to a ball that bounced higher than expected off a shortish length and, with obvious frustration, saw the ball clip the underside of his bat and sail through for a comfortable catch to Gilchrist.

Bell now joined a comfortable-looking Strauss and, with a positive approach, looked to pick up the pace of the scoring, but, with just 44 on the board, he was trapped in front by the ever-reliable Clark for just 7.

That brought Collingwood prematurely to the middle in a certain amount of trouble but, with Strauss continuing his good form, together they managed to settle down the England innings and take the score past 50.

With all of the Australian bowlers keeping to a tight line and good length scoring was proving to be a slow process and, just when, as an England fan, you might have been forgiven for thinking that things were turning your way, the pressure that the Australians had maintained brought dividends. Lee, producing a quick, bouncy delivery, caught Collingwood by surprise and, before he could react differently, he found himself awkwardly fending it off the back foot. The ball then flew off the edge

EARLY STRIKE: Lee is congratulated after claiming the wicket of Cook

OUT OF TOUCH: For the first time Pietersen struggles a little for timing

to Ponting for a smartly judged chance to put England in trouble at 101-3.

Pietersen then came to the middle in an attempt to restore some order to proceedings but no sooner had he arrived, Strauss, after reaching his half century, was to become the historic 700th victim of Warne's illustrious career as, in a effort to drive him through mid-on he was beaten by both length, flight and turn that saw the ball pass between bat and pad to bowl him for 50.

Now Flintoff, looking to repeat his positive approach at the WACA, strove to put bat to ball but, still struggling for form, found scoring tricky and after a brief stay at the crease was caught by Warne at first slip from a probing Clark for 13.

England were now a worrying 122-5 as the replacement wicket-keeper Read came to the middle. Anxious to put runs on the board and keen to establish his place in the team, he was to fall victim to Warne early on as he drove a ball on the up on the off side to Ponting at short cover for 4.

Pietersen now found himself in the familiar position of partnering

the tail and, looking frustrated at his predicament, was soon a further team-mate down as Mahmood offered a regulation catch to Gilchrist off McGrath for 0.

Harmison, now promoted up the order, looked to score a few lusty blows but, as could be considered customary, soon fell victim to his extravagant exploits as, from a wide Warne delivery, Harmison attempted to pull the ball high over mid-on but succeeded only in making a thick contact and sending it straight into the safe hands of Clarke for 7.

Now running out of partners, Pietersen looked to get after the bowling but, looking a little short of his natural timing, in his first effort at launching Warne out of the ground, found himself falling short of the straight boundary and into the reliable hands of Symonds for 21.

That left the two last batsmen at the crease and, although a certain amount of resilience was shown, it wasn't long before Warne was to grab his 5th of the innings. In a remarkable day that had seen the great leg spinner surpass all possible expectations as a Test bowler, the script writer for Warne's career was to complete the story with final figures of 5-39 as England were dismissed for a hugely disappointing 159.

With such a small first-innings total, England were keen for an early wicket. However, despite some aggressive first efforts and some unfortunate decisions, England found themselves at the

mercy of a focused and positive partnership that, in no time, moved to 44.

Eventually, Flintoff tempted Langer into an expansive shot outside off stump and, with huge delight, he saw the ball clip off the edge of the bat for a dipping catch to Read behind the stumps.

With just ten minutes before the close of play, Ponting chose to send Lee into the middle as nightwatchman but, soon after, he was to regret his decision as, one ball later, Flintoff produced a cracker of a delivery to take him to hat-trick ball as a lifting ball outside off stump caught the edge of Lee's bat through to Read for 0.

Australia then survived the last couple of minutes to finish off a marvellous day's entertainment to close on 48-2.

STILL IN IT: Flintoff watches the edge off Langer's bat safely into the gloves of Read

Brisbane

Adelaide

Perth

Melbourne

Sydney

View from the Boundary

ASHES *frontline*

MAGIC MOMENT: Shane Warne and team-mates celebrate the historic 700th Test wicket

Brisbane

Adelaide

Perth

Melbourne

Sydney

Tuesday
26 December 2006

FOURTH TEST, DAY ONE

Both captains (below) wanted to lose the toss. It was one of those days that looked made for bowling, but in the final analysis you always bat and I believe Freddie made the right decision – and the one Ricky Ponting would have made – when the coin fell his way.

People will say he made a bad decision because we were all out for 159. The wicket was a little bit damp and there was rain about. But when it started to rain the toss had been made and play was under way.

England always seem to win the toss in such situations and you can't envy the captain his decision. If we had batted better Freddie wouldn't have been criticised and if he had put Australia in and they had made 400 the knives would have been out.

At the end of the day Freddie's decision backfired because we didn't hang in there when it was tough and get enough runs on the board. It was the positive decision to make and I believe the right one.

It was a magical day for Shane as he became the first bowler to take 700 Test wickets and the ball which bowled Andrew Strauss to take him to the milestone was a corker. The ovation when he came on to bowl was amazing and as usual he delivered.

The Aussie bowlers were putting the ball in good areas, but it was doing so much off the seam that they weren't finding the edge. When that happens you go searching for a wicket and frustration can set in.

It should have been plain sailing from 101-2. Instead Warne came on with the crowd right behind him, got Straussy with a beauty and then tossed a few up to see if we would take the bait. We did and everything he touched turned to gold. He walked off with 5-39 to a standing ovation, but we had contributed much to our own downfall from lunch onwards.

Kevin Pietersen ended up batting with the tail and critics have started to knock the decision to bat him as low as five, although I felt it would be good for him to go in when the

ball was a bit softer and the shine had gone off it. Now I'm not so sure. Your best batsmen in world cricket tend to bat at four or maybe even three, but Kev himself wanted to go in at five and it seemed right for the team we have got and the explosiveness he plays with.

As it turned out, he would ask to go up to four after today's innings and his request was granted, quite rightly. I think he has to stay there. I've batted with him four times now in this series and that is not ideal – unless he is on 180 at the time!

The day ended with Australia 48-2, Freddie having knocked over Justin Langer and nightwatchman Brett Lee with successive balls. Definitely game on as far as we are concerned.

At one point Matthew Hayden whistled across and said: "Hell, this game is going forward." We agreed that we were in for at least one day off at the end.

TOUGH DECISION: Flintoff contemplates his tactics during the coin toss

HERO'S RECEPTION: Warne salutes the crowd on reaching a world-record 700 Test wickets

so when he dismissed Andrew Strauss with another perfect leg spinner, they went absolutely bananas. It was quite incredible being out in the middle of the MCG when 'the king' took his record-breaking wicket. When just under 90,000 people scream and shout their adulation for one of the game's greats the atmosphere is almost surreal.

Backed up by Glenn McGrath, Brett Lee, Stuart Clark and Andrew Symonds, Warney's five-wicket bag was the perfect script for our legend's last Test match on his home soil. Again, our bowlers worked beautifully together leaving us in a very strong position going into day two.

Despite losing yours truly and nightwatchman Brett Lee just ten minutes before stumps, our Boxing Day has been almost perfect. My frustrating summer continued this afternoon but at the end of the day the team had a brilliant day so I can grin and bear the disappointment of throwing away another good start.

Tuesday
26 December 2006

FOURTH TEST, DAY ONE

The moment Andrew Flintoff won the toss and batted first it would be fair to say we were more than a little surprised. While we are not allowed to bet on the game of cricket I would have bet my last dollar that England would bowl first if they won the toss.

In many ways England's bold decision showed enormous courage but by stumps tonight I have to wonder if they are confident they made the right call. Again, our bowling attack was able to rip through England's batting line-up and if we had taken all of our chances then the scorecard might have looked even grimmer for our opponents.

The highlight of the day was Shane Warne's 700th wicket in Test cricket. His home crowd were fired up before he had bowled a ball

NOT FINISHED YET: Warne continues to threaten

Brisbane

Adelaide

Perth

Melbourne

Sydney

View from the Boundary

Wednesday
27 December 2006

FOURTH TEST, DAY TWO

England continued their attack against the Australians with exactly the start they were looking for, having posted such a low first-innings total. Resuming on 48-2 England bowled with real purpose on a pitch that was offering a fair bit to the seamers while the dampness was still in the surface.

Just a dozen runs into the day the big danger man was removed as Ponting, attempting a pull shot from a Flintoff delivery, found himself a little caught out by the 'Tennis Ball' bounce of the MCG and the ball went for a comfortable catch to Cook at mid-wicket.

Hussey then came to the middle and England, keen to remove the next obstacle in the Aussie line-up, were soon celebrating as Hoggard produced a peach of a delivery that went through the normally excellent defence of 'Mr Cricket' to send Australia to 79-4.

GOOD PRESSURE: Ponting feels the heat as England put together a good bowling spell in the first session

Sensing an opportunity, Flintoff brought Harmison into the attack and, just two balls into his spell, Steve produced a sharp, lifting delivery that Clarke could only fend awkwardly through to the wicket-keeper for 5.

84-5 and England were looking at a real chance of dismissing the home side for a total somewhere close to their own and, given Symond's form/average in his Test match history, they would have been forgiven for thinking so. However, he and Hayden, who had battled hard from the start of his innings, had a very different idea.

For the next two sessions and over 200 runs later, both men were still there and, what had begun as

View from the Boundary

IN CONTROL: Hayden issues firm instructions to his partner Symonds on his way to a brilliantly-made 153

Not finishing there, Symmo and his fishing buddy Hayden, settled in to compile another 50 runs each and it wasn't until 30 minutes before the close that Mahmood produced a bouncing and seaming delivery, almost from nowhere, that had Hayden completely turned square to a ball that seamed 3-4 inches towards the slips and caught the edge through to read for a tremendous 153.

Mahmood, now a little buoyed by his first scalp, quickly then picked up the initially vulnerable but dangerous Gilchrist with a 'sucker' ball tossed up outside the left-hander's off stump. Finding the temptation irresistible, Adam swiped wildly at the ball, succeeding only in edging a flashing chance to Collingwood at second slip for just 1.

Warne now received a standing ovation as he walked out for what was likely to be his last innings at the MCG.

England, looking to grab some late-night psychological boost from an otherwise difficult day, then peppered Warne with a series of short balls, but the dogged Victorian held his ground to make it to the close with Symonds at 370-7.

an innings-saving partnership had transformed into a possible match-winning one.

Hayden, with immense concentration on a steadily improving pitch, brought up a fantastic century. Having seen off some early good shouts for lbw he had ridden his luck and grafted out a hugely significant ton.

Symonds, who had entered the middle under huge pressure to dispel his 'One Day' tag as a Test batsman, began playing an innings of much-welcomed maturity. Moving steadily to 50 with ever-increasing confidence on a pitch that rewarded application, he began to blossom with the help of some tiring English bowling and, as the overall total moved from a

position of safety to dominance, it was with tremendous excitement and delight that he brought up his maiden Test century.

SOME WELCOME FORM: Mahmood gets some well deserved results from a useful spell

View from the Boundary

Sydney

Melbourne

Perth

Adelaide

Brisbane

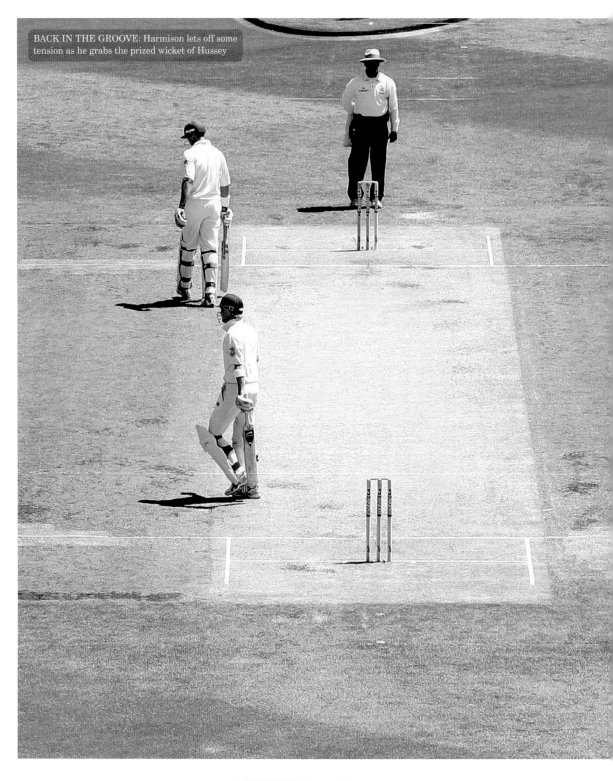

BACK IN THE GROOVE: Harmison lets off some tension as he grabs the prized wicket of Hussey

ASHES *frontline*

Steve Harmison

Wednesday
27 December 2006

FOURTH TEST, DAY TWO

We needed a good start today and we got it. Australia were 84-5 and Andrew Symonds was at the wicket while I bowled three and a half overs at him where I felt I was likely to get him out with every single delivery. I was bowling fast in a decent area and I just kept thinking 'he's bound to nick one in a minute'. It didn't happen and he somehow survived a barrage from both ends.

Like good players do, he bided his time while the bowlers were on top and all credit to him because he has been under a fair bit of pressure. He came out the other side and made a terrific 150, sharing a stand 279 with Hayden, which took the game away from us.

There was criticism of the bowling, but I didn't think it was justified. The difference in the pitch between before lunch and after lunch was immense. The ball went soft, but in any case it didn't do half as much as it had done in the morning session. It dried out and when the sun got on it in the afternoon it played so much better for the batsmen.

It was a bit like Headingley and Lord's back home where, when it is overcast, you think you are going to get a wicket with every ball and when the skies clear and the pitches flatten out it's like bowling on a road.

We had Australia 84-5 so we must have been bowling in good areas and I don't think we changed much after lunch. Hayden and Symonds played very well and had a few moments of fortune that went their way.

The pitch had been difficult to get in on, but they showed that once you were in you could cash in. No other batsman in the match had really reached a position where he could feel comfortable.

When you looked at Australia's score of 372-7 at the end of the day it was made up of only two scores. You have to stay positive and we told ourselves that the wicket had got considerably better.

We knew that even if they got 400-plus if we could match it we would have 150-odd runs to play with when they had to bat last. And we would settle for that after our poor first innings.

I still maintain that we bowled reasonably well throughout the day. Two Australians played exceptionally well, but both had decisions go their way at times when it made a huge difference. The bowlers stuck to their task and didn't get the rub of the green. If we had got it the game might have been 150 playing 200-odd and we would have fancied our chances.

TOUGH GOING: Flintoff discusses tactics with Harmison as the lead begins to grow

Wednesday

27 December 2006

FOURTH TEST, DAY TWO

When Andrew Symonds walked onto the MCG, I can't remember hoping one of my team-mates would score some runs, like I hoped he would today. Not only were we under pressure but I believe Andrew is one of those players who possesses that X factor which makes him an invaluable member of this cricket team.

Unfortunately in the world we live in, statistics like runs and wickets are the only currency of value, and yet, numbers alone rarely tell the whole tale of the value of certain players. I have no doubt Symmo is one of those players and now that he is adding those numbers to his awesome natural ability, we can all breathe a little easier at his prospects of playing more Test cricket.

The beauty and brilliance of Andy Symonds as a team-mate is that he can bat with the brutal authority that he displayed today, he bowls medium pace and off spin, and is also the world's best fieldsman. He also adds character and humour to the changing room and his passion for the baggy green cap and his mates is infectious.

His reaction when he reached his maiden Test century was priceless and considering he was batting with one of his best mates in Matty Hayden it was hard to hold back the tears when the ball sailed 20 rows back into the grandstand. No one has encouraged and supported Symmo like Haydos has, so it was one of those magical moments when the two of them were able to celebrate such a milestone in front of 75,000 people at the MCG.

My opening partner was once again brilliant today as he fought hard for a couple of hours before playing at his belligerent best. His timely century has us in an incredible position of strength after an ordinary start to day two.

From where I was watching the game, I thought England generally bowled far too short and while the pitch looked to have flattened out this afternoon, I wouldn't be surprised if they will have a tough time of batting in their second innings. When the ball was pitched up it still seamed around and I am sure we will be looking to have England's batsmen hitting off the front foot for most of their innings some time tomorrow.

JUST REWARD: Symonds, who had been under much pressure for runs, shows obvious delight with his friend Hayden upon reaching his maiden Test hundred

View from the Boundary

Sydney

Melbourne

Perth

Adelaide

Brisbane

Thursday
28 December 2006

FOURTH TEST, DAY THREE

Australia resumed their innings in the morning with England anxious to dismiss them as quickly as possible, if they were to have any chance in keeping themselves in this game.

Symonds, who had batted so beautifully the day before to pass 150, lasted only a few deliveries as, tempted by a full ball from Harmison, he managed only to edge it through to Read for a magnificent 156.

That was the start the tourists were looking for and, with Clarke and Warne now in the middle, England looked to finish off the tail as soon as possible.

STUBBORN RESISTANCE: Warne hangs around to make a useful 40

With the Australians building their score past a formidable 400, having once been a worrying 84-5, the lead moved past 250 and, with it, the chance of a 4-0 lead became a real possibility.

Mahmood then, bowling with good pace, managed to catch the edge of Clark's bat through to Read for 8 to bring McGrath to the middle for his last innings at the MCG.

Unfortunately the standing ovation he received on his way to the middle was to last longer that his innings as Mahmood got him to edge one to gully for his 35th duck of his career.

Australia finished on 419, a useful 260 runs ahead, as England came to the middle with the intention of first saving the game and then, maybe, looking to build a small lead for the Australians to chase on the last day.

However, after a steady start with limited chances from the openers, it was on a disappointing 41 when Cook was to begin the England downfall.

Pushing out at a Clark delivery, Cook played all round a straight one and headed back to the pavilion for just 20.

Bell, once again, now found himself in the middle earlier than he had hoped and, with McGrath bowling his customary line and length in his penultimate Test, it wasn't long before he was heading back to the dressing room after Glen trapped him in front for just 2.

England now, following much criticism of their batting order in the previous games, sent Pietersen to the crease ahead of Collingwood in an attempt to prevent him from running out of top-order partners as the innings progressed.

Well, the theory may have been a good one but, on this occasion, it was to prove fruitless as, just a few deliveries after his arrival, Clark

SHOWING SOME FIGHT: Monty applies himself as best as possible in support of his partner Read

got a ball of good length to seam in a little from just outside the off stump and, as Pietersen attempted a drive through the covers, the Australians leapt in jubilation as the ball passed between bat and pad to bowl him for just 1 and leave England in real trouble at 49-3.

Now Collingwood came to the middle to join Strauss, who was doing his best to hold things together at the other end.

Momentarily the two looked comfortable and moved the score on and, for a short time, began to dampen the raucous atmosphere at the MCG.

However, with the score on just 75, the crowd was to be ignited again as Collingwood drove Lee on the up through the covers and, in a trap set deliberately for that shot, hit the ball straight to Langer for a sharp catch and finish his brief spell in the middle on 16.

A SPORTING REUNION: Lee shakes the hand of Freddie as the victor on this occasion

The captain and vice-captain now shouldered the responsibility of saving the game and the embarrassment of losing inside three days.

Flintoff, again looking to 'hit' his way into form, began to accrue some runs, albeit a little 'clumsily' but it was Strauss who was to depart next. Lee, bowling an aggressive spell, got one to lift off a decent length and Strauss could do nothing but get a slight nick on it through to Gilchrist for 31.

Now 90-5 and facing defeat, Flintoff was joined by Read but, after having edged just past the 100 mark, he too was to fall victim to the impressive Australian bowling attack, as he was adjudge lbw to Clark for 25.

England were now firmly into the tail with Mahmood batting alongside the wicket-keeper and, as might be expected, it was to be a brief liaison as, just one run later,

Warne had Mahmood playing inside to a ball that went straight on and flicked his pad in front of off stump, leaving him lbw for 0.

Panesar now looked to improve upon his country's resistance but, after the addition of a determined 18 runs, Harmison fell the same way as his previous fast-bowling team-mate as Warne got one past his defences to strike him on the toe and fall lbw for 4.

England were now down to 127-8 and staring at a humiliating fourth consecutive defeat. Monty, showing further resilience, attempted to play the occasional stroke in support of Read who, given the circumstances, had amassed an impressive 20 runs.

However, yet again, he was to be left watching another partner depart as Lee, with his added pace and bounce, got Monty fending one in an ugly fashion off his face to a ball he assumed would bounce harmlessly over him but, instead, he ended up spooning it to Clarke in the gully for the simplest of dismissals.

Now 146-9, the tourists were on the brink of defeat and, with a

swelling Melbourne crowd anxious to see the victory and their departing heroes Warne and McGrath, they were not made to wait long as on 161, just two runs more than their first innings, Lee got one to duck into Hoggard off a Yorker length and removed his leg stump for 5.

Australia completed a tremendous day with a victory of an innings and 99 runs in which they had continued to out-play England in every department of the game.

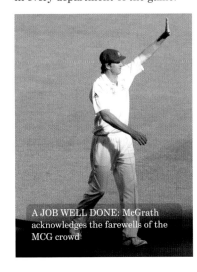

A JOB WELL DONE: McGrath acknowledges the farewells of the MCG crowd

Brisbane

Adelaide

Perth

Melbourne

Sydney

INTO THE TRAP: Collingwood looks on as he drives the ball straight to Langer at short cover

Brisbane • Adelaide • Perth • Melbourne • Sydney

Steve Harmison

Sydney

Melbourne

Perth

Adelaide

Brisbane

Thursday
28 December 2006

FOURTH TEST, DAY THREE

I had been happy with the way I bowled on day two and that feeling continued today as I managed to get Symonds caught behind, having added only two to his overnight score. I finished with 2-69 from 28 overs in an Australian total of 419 and just felt the progress I had made since the Brisbane debacle had been continued.

I had improved considerably at Adelaide without getting the wickets I thought I deserved and then took wickets at Perth to confirm that I was a different bowler to the one who had sent down that infamous first delivery of the series.

Now I feel I have come full circle. Here I have bowled in an area, rather than striving too much for dismissals, which as I said before you can tend to do when the ball is moving around off the pitch.

It's so easy to get frustrated, vary your length, and end up going for six or seven an over by being cut and pulled.

I started well in this game and kept on a roll, trying to bowl dot balls and maidens. I'd have liked more wickets, but I felt I did my job for the team in keeping the run-rate down and I was pleased with my performance.

Saj Mahmood has ended up with 4-100 for a timely confidence booster following some remarks in a newspaper article claiming he had been under-bowled by the skipper in the previous Test.

I must admit I looked at his newspaper comments and thought 'what have you said', because we didn't need that sort of thing as a team. Perhaps Saj was a bit naïve and maybe he got stitched up, but I feel we have stuck together as a side on this trip in the face of a lot of criticism so his comments were disappointing.

Unfortunately, we couldn't get near the sort of total we hoped for to stay in the game and 161 all out just confirmed we are in a rut and all too likely to capitulate once two or three wickets are down.

Looking back I think the defeat in the second Test at Adelaide, when a draw looked certain, took more out of us than we could admit at the time. In the previous series winning the second Test at Edgbaston gave us a massive, positive knock-on effect, having lost the first Test. This time the opposite was true.

Once more we were unable to rise to the challenge they threw at us and to lose in three days was another miserable experience.

Freddie took a lot more stick as a result, but he shouldn't shoulder the blame. Not many of us have performed and I hold my hand up to being one of those who has not done well enough. Freddie was and is the right man to captain this team. He remains the larger than life character we all look up to and aspire to match as a person and a player.

I wouldn't say we have let him down because we have tried our best, but I do feel sorry for him as a friend and a colleague because no skipper could have done more.

He has tried his nuts off from day one and it's not his fault we aren't winning. We are being beaten by a better team.

I don't think the captaincy weighs him down when he is batting or bowling. He bats as a batsman and bowls as a bowler, only putting his skipper's hat on in between. Whoever had been our captain in this series I believe we would still be 4-0 down. Now all that is left to us is to avoid 5-0 and that means a hell of a lot.

I think there is only me left from the team who faced this position before, although Hoggy played in the last Test at Sydney where we arrived facing a whitewash. We haven't played well in this series, but we were ten times worse on that last trip here and everyone expected a whitewash. In fact, we won and we certainly don't want to finish this series on the end of a 5-0 so we will apply ourselves as professionally as we can and try to turn the tide.

LATE CONSOLATION: Harmison finally gets the wicket of Symonds for a tremendous 156 as Shane Warne looks on

Thursday
28 December 2006

FOURTH TEST, DAY THREE

Yesterday it was my view England bowled too short to Andrew Symonds and Matty Hayden. This in mind our objective today was a simple one. Ricky instructed our bowlers to pitch the ball up and be very disciplined and he asked all the fieldsmen to field with energy and enthusiasm and to jump on everything so that England knew we meant business.

By about 6pm it would be fair to say that this disciplined approach had paid dividends and as we walked off the MCG for the last time with Shane Warne and Glenn

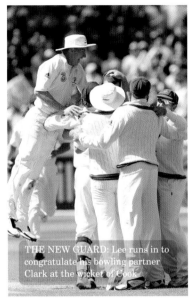

THE NEW GUARD: Lee runs in to congratulate his bowling partner Clark at the wicket of Cook

McGrath, we felt pleased with another job well done.

It is hard to describe the emotions of seeing the back of two legends and I am guessing next week in Sydney will be tough, but the drama has been easier because of the attitude the two of them

have taken since their decisions became public. They have approached this last Test as if it were their first and both of them bowled brilliantly throughout. They also seem so relaxed and at ease and as a result the feeling within our changing rooms is fantastic.

Brett Lee and Stuart Clark backed up the retirees perfectly today and once again the four of them pulled off another amazing team effort. The thought of winning this fourth Test match in three days is amazing and I must admit it brought back memories of those glory days when we won 16 straight Test matches, where most of them were over in three days.

Never could I have imagined this series would have been won so comprehensively and now with one Test to go we know we have an opportunity to realize our pre-series ambition of a clean sweep. The England guys didn't come into our rooms for a beer tonight. I guess they feel like they have hit rock bottom.

A FOND FAREWELL: Warne emotionally departs the MCG for the last time

Scorecard

England 1st Innings

			Runs	Balls	4s	6s
A J Strauss		b S K Warne	50	132	2	0
A N Cook	c A C Gilchrist	b B Lee	11	37	0	0
I R Bell	lbw	b S R Clark	7	30	0	0
P D Collingwood	c R T Ponting	b B Lee	28	82	4	0
K P Pietersen	c A Symonds	b S K Warne	21	70	0	0
A Flintoff	c S K Warne	b S R Clark	13	31	1	0
C M W Read	c R T Ponting	b S K Warne	3	17	0	0
S I Mahmood	c A C Gilchrist	b G D McGrath	0	9	0	0
S J Harmison	c M J Clarke	b S K Warne	7	12	1	0
M S Panesar	c A Symonds	b S K Warne	4	19	0	0
M J Hoggard	not out		9	10	1	0
Extras		3nb 2b 1lb	6			
Total		all out	159	(74.2 ovs)		

Bowling	O	M	R	W
B Lee	13	4	36	2
G D McGrath	20	8	37	1
S R Clark	17	6	27	2
A Symonds	7	2	17	0
S K Warne	17.2	4	39	5

Fall of wicket

23 (A N Cook), 44 (I R Bell), 101 (P D Collingwood),
101 (A J Strauss), 122 (A Flintoff), 135 (C M W Read),
136 (S I Mahmood), 145 (S J Harmison), 146 (K P Pietersen),
159 (M S Panesar)

Australia 1st Innings

			Runs	Balls	4s	6s
J L Langer	c C M W Read	b A Flintoff	27	29	3	0
M L Hayden	c C M W Read	b S I Mahmood	153	265	13	2
B Lee	c C M W Read	b A Flintoff	0	1	0	0
R T Ponting	c C N Cook	b A Flintoff	7	28	0	0
M E K Hussey		b M J Hoggard	6	20	0	0
M J Clarke	c C M W Read	b S J Harmison	5	5	0	0
A Symonds	c C M W Read	b S J Harmison	156	220	15	1
A C Gilchrist	c P D Collingwood	b S I Mahmood	1	8	0	0
S K Warne	not out		40	54	6	0
S R Clark	c C M W Read	b S I Mahmood	8	24	0	0
G D McGrath	c I R Bell	b S I Mahmood	0	6	0	0
Extras		9nb 1w 6lb	16			
Total		all out	419	(108.3 ovs)		

Bowling	O	M	R	W
M J Hoggard	21	6	82	1
A Flintoff	22	1	77	3
S J Harmison	28	6	69	2
S I Mahmood	21.3	1	100	4
M S Panesar	12	1	52	0
P D Collingwood	3	0	20	0
K P Pietersen	1	0	13	0

Fall of wicket

44 (J L Langer), 44 (B Lee), 62 (R T Ponting), 79 (M E K
Hussey), 84 (M J Clarke), 363 (M L Hayden), 365 (A C Gilchrist),
383 (A Symonds), 417 (S R Clark), 419 (G D McGrath)

England 2nd Innings

			Runs	Balls	4s	6s
A J Strauss	c A C Gilchrist	b B Lee	31	107	2	0
A N Cook		b S R Clark	20	46	1	0
I R Bell	lbw	b G D McGrath	2	11	0	0
K P Pietersen		b S R Clark	1	8	0	0
P D Collingwood	c J L Langer	b B Lee	16	38	0	0
A Flintoff	lbw	b S R Clark	25	45	2	0
C M W Read	not out		26	77	1	0
S I Mahmood	lbw	b S K Warne	0	2	0	0
S J Harmison	lbw	b S K Warne	4	26	0	0
M S Panesar	c M J Clarke	b B Lee	14	19	2	0
M J Hoggard		b B Lee	5	20	0	0
Extras		4nb 1w 12lb	17			
Total		all out	161	(65.5 ovs)		

Bowling	O	M	R	W
B Lee	18.5	6	47	4
G D McGrath	12	2	26	1
S R Clark	16	6	30	3
S K Warne	19	3	46	2

Fall of wicket

41 (A N Cook), 48 (I R Bell), 49 (K P Pietersen),
75 (P D Collingwood), 90 (A J Strauss), 108 (A Flintoff),
109 (S I Mahmood), 127 (S J Harmison), 146 (M S Panesar),
161 (M J Hoggard)

Australia beat England by an Innings and 99 runs

Brisbane

Adelaide

Perth

Melbourne

Sydney

FIFTH TEST
Sydney
Sydney Cricket Ground

Sydney

Melbourne

Perth

Adelaide

Brisbane

Teams

Umpires: Aleem Dar, B F Bowden

Australia: J L Langer, M L Hayden, R T Ponting, M E K Hussey, M J Clarke, A Symonds, A C Gilchrist, S K Warne, B Lee, S R Clark, G D McGrath

England: A J Strauss, A N Cook, I R Bell, K P Pietersen, P D Collingwood, A Flintoff, C M W Read, S I Mahmood, S J Harmison, J M Anderson, M S Panesar

England won the toss and elected to bat

SERVED THEIR COUNTRY WELL: McGrath, Langer and Warne enter the Test arena for the last time

Tuesday

02 January 2007

FIFTH TEST, DAY ONE

Not for over three quarters of a century has an England side lost the Ashes by a whitewash and this England side were keen not to be the next.

Andrew Flintoff began by getting the first decision of the day correct when, on a pretty flat batting surface, he won the toss and elected to bat.

Although a little bit of greenness showed on the surface and the ball was seaming a little for Glen McGrath and Brett Lee, both the openers got off to a steady start.

Anxious to establish a decent first-innings total, Strauss and Cook, following a 45-minute delay for rain, played with good concentration and patience against some beautifully tight and disciplined bowling from the Australians. Slowly they progressed the score and began to look settled until, just after setting their best partnership of the series, Strauss looked to cut a quick ball from Lee that was perhaps a little too full to warrant the shot and, a tad late on the stroke, managed only to get a top edge on the ball and send through an easy catch to Gilchrist.

England were now 45-1 as Bell came to the middle and, with Lee and Clark bowling well in tandem, both players added a dozen runs to the total as they went into the break.

Keeping the ever-dangerous Clark on after the interval, Ponting's decision was to prove correct as, no sooner had the two England batsmen resumed their innings, Cook drove at one just outside the off stump and got an inside edge on it through to

TUCKED UP: Strauss narrowly avoids a quick ball from Lee

position to play the stroke, McGrath's miser-like approach paid off as the ball sailed to Hussey at mid-wicket for a well-judged catch.

Pietersen was gone for 41 and the score was now 166-3 as Collingwood came to the crease to partner Bell. However, Collingwood was soon to be greeting a new partner as McGrath, anxious to perform well in his last Test match, produced a peach of a delivery that seamed in off a full length to bowl Bell through the gate for a well-made 71.

In the space of just two overs England had slumped from a healthy 166-2 to a concerning 167-4 as Flintoff joined Collingwood in an attempt to ensure this mini-collapse was not to be the start of something disastrous.

Again, for the third innings in succession, Flintoff began edgily as he struggled for fluency with the bat but, supported by the ever-determined and dogged competitor Collingwood grinding out runs at the other end, Flintoff, having battled through the early overs of his innings, looked to impose his natural strength against the attack.

Gaining confidence as time went on, Flintoff struck some powerful blows to progress his score to 42 and with Collingwood steadily amassing 25 at the other end, England went into the dressing room on a relatively comfortable 234-4 by the close of play.

Gilchrist. Adam, adjusting well to take the ball down the leg side, sent England to a worrying 58-2 as the newly-promoted Pietersen came to the middle.

Then, albeit at a reasonably slow scoring rate, the two began to accrue a useful partnership and steer their country back into a healthier position. Bell, as watchful as ever, moved his score past 50 for the fourth time in the series as Pietersen, stifled somewhat by the accuracy and consistency of the Australian attack, contained his natural aggression to support the number three as, together, they moved the score past the hundred mark.

Eventually Pietersen's patience was to be pushed too far and, in spotting a rare shorter-length delivery from McGrath, he attempted to pull the ball through square leg. However, not quite in

FIGHTING BACK: Warne ponders a different approach as England build a useful partnership

View from the Boundary

UNFALTERING SUPPORT: Cheerful and as raucous as ever, the Barmy Army cheer their team along

Sydney

Melbourne

Perth

Adelaide

Brisbane

Tuesday
02 January 2007

FIFTH TEST, DAY ONE

The team talk before the game centred around us having been 4-0 down in the series the last time we got to Sydney and, with a team I consider to have been a lot worse than our current side.

The way they have approached this series, there was never much chance of them losing focus and our task was always going to be far more difficult. But it was a positive thought we could take in to the match.

Again we won the toss and again it wasn't the easiest of decisions to bat first because there was rain about and conditions early on were always going to favour the bowlers.

ANOTHER GOOD START: Bell acknowledges his team-mates upon reaching fifty

There was great atmosphere in the ground because the Barmy Army were all in one area, which enabled them to make a lot of noise. The Aussie fans were as hostile and in your face as they had been in the previous four Tests so, despite the series score, there was a real sense of excitement going into the match.

The Barmy Army have been awesome for us since day one in Brisbane. Even in Perth where Australia regained the Ashes they were singing their hearts out and kept going even while the Aussies were doing their lap of honour. One thing that will stick with me about this tour is how the England fans kept behind us.

We don't get a lot of chance to talk to them as individuals so this is a good chance to express how much they mean to the players. They appreciate good cricket from both sides and we are proud of them wherever we go around the world. They are the best fans in sport in my opinion. I cannot say more than that. In other sports the fans would have disowned the team the way results have gone on this trip.

We knew the ball would nip about a bit early on and again Australia bowled well as a unit. But our batsmen applied themselves well, stood firm and stuck to their plans. We said we didn't want to lose 5-0 and we wanted to go out there and prove it. Unfortunately, we lost Andrew Strauss and Nick Cook either side of lunch, which gave Australia a lift at important times, but Ian Bell went on to make 71, again proving that he can make runs against the best bowlers in the world. I wouldn't say he arrived with scars from the last meeting with Australia, but the one thing Belly wanted to show on this trip was that he could succeed against the top side in the world. He played

FIRST ONE DOWN: Lee sees off Strauss for 29

a number of fine innings in the series and will just be disappointed that he didn't kick on to a hundred enough times. Despite that, he has been one of the plusses for us.

KP had done his best to get McGrath off his usual exemplary line and length during the series by using his feet to him and coming down the wicket. It upset McGrath quite a bit, but like all great bowlers he had an answer. Just as Kev was working himself into a position to really have a go he was out for 41, miscuing a short-ball, having advanced to meet it.

Paul Collingwood played solidly again and the efforts of the top order batsmen for once allowed Andrew Flintoff to come in at six with a bit of licence to play his shots.

At the end of the day, with the score 234-4 and Freddie going well, we probably had the happier dressing room, something we can't claim often in this series.

Tuesday
02 January 2007

FIFTH TEST, DAY ONE

Yesterday at a press conference I announced my retirement from Test cricket. As hard as it was to finally let go of the opportunity to wear the baggy green cap after this final Test, I know in my heart that I have done the right thing. Many people have guaranteed me that I would know when the time was right and while I have fought not to let it go, the feeling came to me on Saturday morning.

It is difficult to describe such a feeling but it was as if all the thoughts about my future that have been running wild in my mind for the last week or so travelled from my head to my heart. Like so many big decisions in your life as soon as the feeling reached my heart the deal was sealed and although it was tough telling my family and my team-mates, particularly Ricky and Matty Hayden, it felt like a load had been lifted off my shoulders the moment the decision was made.

While I think I have held my emotions together pretty well, this morning was a sad time. Instead of jumping out of my skin to enjoy this, my last Test, I felt like crying the whole morning. First during the national anthem ceremony I started to get a bit teary. Then when I looked up to one of the corporate suites to where my family was sitting, the lump started rising again in my throat. Finally as I stood from my corner of the changing room to walk out onto the field I could hardly contain myself. Every time I looked at Haydos, Ricky or Adam Gilchrist and I realized this would be the last time I would play with these, my

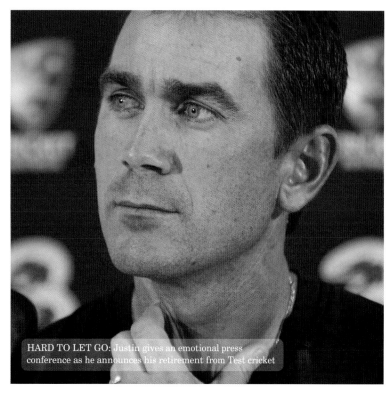

HARD TO LET GO: Justin gives an emotional press conference as he announces his retirement from Test cricket

best friends, I had to fight back the tears.

For the last two days I have read many tributes on my career and most of them have mentioned descriptions like a tough fighter who has battled hard for his country. This morning I felt more like an emotional little girl than the picture that has been painted of me. I guess if playing for Australia didn't mean so much to me then it wouldn't be so hard to let it go but wearing the baggy green cap has been my dream since I was a young boy, and my life for the last fourteen years.

Knowing this is my last Test is a little surreal, and it took me at least the first session to click into something close to normal business mode this morning. Dropping Andrew Strauss at third slip snapped me back to reality but until that moment I was away with

the fairies. I couldn't turn off the emotions or sentiments and I felt lost in the lonely space of my own world which is definitely not where you want to be when you are involved in an Ashes contest at the Sydney cricket ground.

Tonight I feel exhausted, not by the 87 overs in the field but rather by the time I spent with the conflicting emotions of playing my last Test. On paper, some may feel England had the better of day one, but considering Andrew Flintoff won the toss and batted first, we are happy with the state of play at stumps. With the new ball due first thing in the morning I can't help but think that England's slow run rate today has kept us in the game once again.

Removing England's skipper will be our highest priority when another emotional day gets under way in the morning.

View from the Boundary

Wednesday
03 January 2007

FIFTH TEST, DAY TWO

England resumed their innings in the morning hopeful of a score in excess of 350. With the pitch offering a little to the seamers the tourists would have been hopeful to defend such a target.

However, the Australian bowling attack, once again, bowled well as a unit, applying huge pressure to the England batsmen from both ends.

With the score having moved on to just 245 Collingwood was to become the first of three victims to fall in quick succession as, cramped for room by the metronome-like accuracy of McGrath, he finally edged one through to the keeper for 27.

Read then came to the middle to join Flintoff, who was beginning to find some nice touch at the other end, but he was soon to depart as Lee, bowling with improved rhythm in this Test, found the edge of his bat for another Gilchrist scalp.

Now England entered the beginning of a long tail and whilst they would have hoped it would 'wag' for them to take the total past 300, Lee was to have Mahmood the very next delivery, edging the ball to the safe hands of Hayden in the gully.

At 258-7, and with a hat-trick ball to face, Harmison joined his good mate Flintoff in the middle with the intention of sticking around long enough for his partner to add some valuable runs. With Freddie striking the ball nicely, the pair worked the field well for the next 30 minutes and whilst Flintoff protected his partner from the majority of the strike, he scored relatively freely to push his total into the eighties.

Eventually, after a small partnership of 24, Harmison missed

FLAT OUT: Monty attempts to stop a firmly hit on-drive from his own bowling

WELCOME RUNS: Flintoff is congratulated on reaching a fluent fifty

a straight Yorker-length full toss and was given lbw for a useful and resilient 2 runs.

Flintoff, now partnered by Panesar, looked to get on with things as he began to run out of team-mates but, perhaps inevitably, his extravagance was to get the better of him and just 9 runs later he came down the wicket to a good-length delivery from Clark and, falling a little short of getting to the pitch of it, his attempted full-blooded swing to deep long off became a thick edge towards Shane Warne at first slip, intercepted on its path by a quick-reacting Gilchrist for a well made 89.

That brought the last England pair together at 291-9 and although both Panesar and Andersen looked

together they began to score fluently against some well-meaning but ultimately, untroubling deliveries.

However, with his team just reaching the hundred mark, Harmison was to tempt him with a wide one outside off stump and with obvious annoyance at being suckered into his 'Achilles' heel' of a shot, the ball came off a thick edge to Collingwood at second slip for a sharp catch.

Now with Australia 100-2 and facing Hussey, and Ponting looking in his usual good form, England could have been fearful that their small total might be made to look that way but, quite uncharacteristically, Ricky pushed a Monty Panesar delivery down to Anderson at mid-off for a sharp single. Alert to the possibility of the captain's misjudgement, Anderson moved quickly to the ball and, with a quickly-released direct hit, left Ponting a good six inches short of his ground to dismiss him for a confident 45.

At 118-3 the momentum of the game was just beginning to turn a little in the tourists' favour and, lifted by the chance of keeping Australia to a sensible total, the English bowled with purpose and aggression on a pitch that, as the collection of mid-level scores had suggested so far in the match, was one that always offered something to the bowlers who were prepared to bend their backs and remain disciplined.

Passing the edge of the bat on a few occasions both Monty and Harmison were short of luck as Clarke and Hussey began to pick up the scoring a little. However, their patience was to be eventually rewarded as, on 155, Harmison finally got the edge he'd been looking for as Clarke, looking to cut a ball that bounced steeply on him, was cramped for room and sent a

comfortable catch through to Read for 11.

As Symonds was making his way into the middle to face a now buoyed England team, to his relief the clouds quickly moved over the SCG and, by the time he had reached the wicket, he was to find himself joining the others on the way back in for a delay in play.

Some 45 minutes later, play resumed and England, keen to make something of the 30 minutes or so before the end of play, bowled with aggression and commitment.

Symonds and Hussey, knowing the importance of seeing off the last few overs, retracted a little into their shells and, with maturity and patience, survived to ensure they would both be back at the crease in the morning.

SEEING OUT THE DAY: Hussey plays watchfully in his efforts to make the close of play

focused, their intentions were not to match their ability as just one over later Monty attempted to sweep a full-length delivery from Warne and, upon missing it, was to provide Shane with his 1000th first-class wicket of his illustrious career.

Australia began their innings with Langer, in his final Test match, looking to get his country off to a positive start. Opening with Anderson and Flintoff, England found the total moving on at a worrying pace before, having scored 26 from just 27 deliveries, Anderson had Langer caught behind with the score on 34.

Hayden, now with Ponting, resumed command of the scoring now that his more aggressive partner had been dismissed and

View from the Boundary

LAST STAND: McGrath continues his last few spells of Test-match bowling at his home ground

ASHES *frontline*

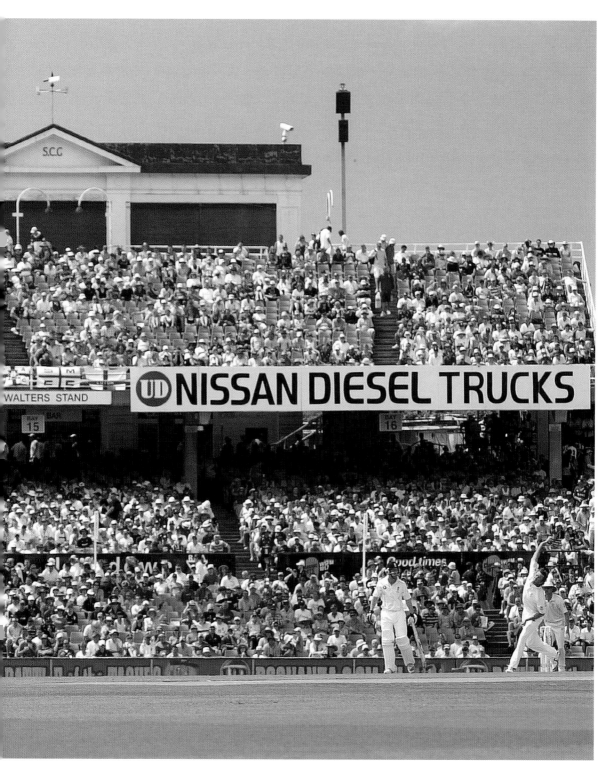

Brisbane

Adelaide

Perth

Melbourne

Sydney

Wednesday

03 January 2007

FIFTH TEST, DAY TWO

This morning we didn't lose any play, but it was still damp and overcast – and Australia had a new ball to operate with. It was always going to do a bit and, the way our tail has batted throughout the series, we knew much depended on the overnight partnership of Colly and Fred.

It was broken early by a typical bit of bowling from McGrath, who nipped two or three balls back off the seam at Colly and then managed to make one go the other way to attract a thin edge through to Adam Gilchrist. From then on the job of all of us still to bat was to support Fred and we failed to do it to the best of our ability.

HIGH FLYER: Lee celebrates two quick wickets for Australia

Brett Lee bowled a fiery spell to remove Chris Read and then Saj Mahmood first ball. At that point in walked yours truly with his big mate at the other end and Fred doesn't do my confidence a lot of good by coming to meet me and saying: "He's bowling bloody quickly! It's coming down with something on it." Not exactly what I wanted to hear, but that's Fred, always honest. Fortunately, the ball was not brand spanking new and I knew Lee would only aim at two places, my head and my toes. So I was quite happy with that and managed to hang around for getting on for an hour.

Andrew prefers to take as much of the strike as possible, reasoning that if he takes the first three or four balls of an over and the field is then brought in, he has more chance of hitting boundaries than I have.

I was eventually out lbw to Clark, a decision I felt was fair enough at the time, even though Freddie showed his disappointment. When I got back to the dressing room and saw TV replays suggesting the ball might just have clipped leg-stump I realised it was another tail-ender's decision.

A total of 291 all out was more than disappointing from our overnight position because we were hoping for a score that at least would make defeat unlikely. It was nowhere near what we needed.

Justin Langer came out blazing in his final Test and I helped his cause with my first two balls, slipping on the front crease first up and then sending down a terrible second delivery.

It seemed I was joining the party. Justin was clearly looking to end his Test career on a high and appeared to be doing just that when he managed to nick one down the leg side off Jimmy Anderson and Chris Read took the catch.

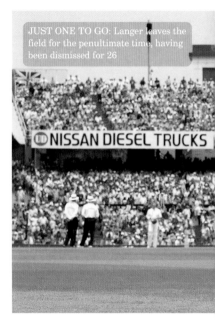

JUST ONE TO GO: Langer leaves the field for the penultimate time, having been dismissed for 26

That got us going and I followed up by having Matt Hayden caught at second slip by Paul Collingwood to make it 100-2.

We then had the great bonus of running out Ricky Ponting as he tried a quick single to mid-on off Monty Panesar. Often fast bowlers are put out to graze at mid-on or fine-leg in between spells and aren't as interested as they might be in what's going on in the game. But Jimmy is different because he is quite a decent backward-point and one of our better fielders. Ponting was trying as always to be positive, but picked the wrong fielder.

It was 155-4 when I managed to get Michael Clarke out just before a break for rain, which I'm sure infuriated him. We went off at the fall of the wicket so it was a great time to break through.

I did the press conference at the close of play and all the talk was of what a good game was developing with us holding a lead of 103. The first session the next morning looked like being crucial.

Wednesday
03 January 2007

FIFTH TEST, DAY TWO

One thing I have learned from today is that you should never tempt the fate of the cricket gods. In my press conference the other day I declared that I had been catching and fielding better than ever. This feeling has been backed up by the fact that I have taken a number of very good catches this summer.

Obviously the gods who act to keep players grounded, decided to teach me a lesson as I spilled three chances in England's first innings. To be fair, the first one this morning off Paul Collingwood was a tough one but the second off Monty Panesar was an absolute sitter.

It was like my 100th Test match in Johannesburg. In the lead up the accolades and tributes I had received had me floating with pride and yet when my time came to bat,

I faced just one ball before being knocked out by a brutal bouncer. The gods were warning me not to get too carried away with my success and to literally keep my eye on the ball or suffer the consequences.

Back then I did, just as I did today. The game of cricket is all about the ball and if you get distracted and lose your concentration then the price will be paid. In Johannesburg the price was a painful one, today I felt like digging a hole and burying myself, as the third chance went down.

As luck would have it we had to go out and bat for one over before lunch. Having dropped three catches I couldn't help but think I was in for another tormenting lesson by being dismissed in that horrible little time to bat. For an opening batsman there is no worse time to bat other than just before stumps but thankfully today I was able to get through an Andrew Flintoff over and walk off a relieved man.

Unfortunately my relief didn't last that long as I was out for 26, caught for the first time in my Test career down the leg side off my

glove. It is impossible to put into words how frustrated I am feeling at the moment. I am hitting the ball so well and yet the results show nothing more than a number of starts. If it wasn't my last Test match I could have easily have been found hanging from the rafters, half an hour after I was out.

As predicted yesterday the new ball paid dividends for us this morning and despite my dropped catches we dismissed the last six England wickets for just over fifty runs. Our bowlers have been relentless this series and again they made the most of a lively SCG wicket to keep us well and truly in the game.

Traditionally this surface gets tougher and tougher to bat on, so our first innings is going to be of vital importance to the result of this game. Ricky Ponting's run out was critical but with Michael Hussey and Andrew Symonds at the crease we will be looking to eke out every single run we can tomorrow. The game is set for an exciting finale and with two days complete I believe the honours are pretty even tonight.

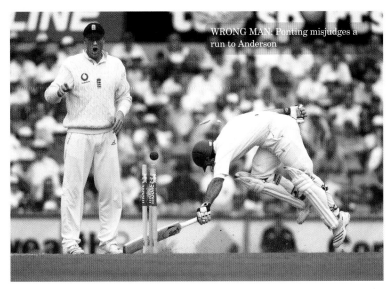

WRONG MAN: Ponting misjudges a run to Anderson

Thursday

04 January 2007

FIFTH TEST, DAY THREE

Australia, keen to establish a first-innings lead in this game, got off to a bad start as Hussey, without adding to his overnight total, drove at a full length ball angled across his off stump and got a thin edge for a well-judged dipping catch to Read for 37.

That brought Gilchrist to the crease and with it the ever present danger of a flurry of runs. However, conscious that his team had a little work to do, both he and Symonds batted with restraint, and with the help of some helpful field placings began to steadily progress their total up towards that of England.

After the seamers had each completed a brief spell without further success, Flintoff threw the ball to Monty and almost immediately he extracted a little life out of the pitch, and with it heightened the air of expectation around the packed SCG.

Beating the bat on a couple of occasions, he bowled without much luck as both Symonds and Gilchrist began to look comfortable on this occasionally unpredictable surface.

Eventually as Australia closed in on England's total and Symonds in on his fifty, he was undone by the flight of a Monty delivery and, in attempting a solid drive through the off side, he was beaten by the ball and bowled for a decent 48.

That brought Warne to the crease and, as usual, an increased sense of excitement around the ground. Quickly into his stride and perhaps keen to make an impression on what might be his last Test innings, Warne hit Monty high over mid-wicket for six, and

although soon after he survived a decent claim for caught behind, looked in confident mood.

Gilchrist, now with the England's first-innings score reached, began to open his shoulders and, with a series of clean strikes, progressed quickly to his fifty.

Together the two players were scoring at more than a run a ball and both looked to be in good form when, soon after taking the new ball, upon reaching for a wide Anderson delivery, Gilchrist made contact with the ground as he attempted to square drive and, as the ball passed through into Read's gloves, the umpire, to Adam's obvious surprise, adjudged him to have made contact and gave him out for a fluent 62.

England, now with Australia on 318-7 and just 27 runs ahead, looked to grab another wicket or two before the interval but Warne, in belligerent mood, was having none of it as he and Lee took Australia into the break on 325.

With just a small lead on the English the tourists were lifted further just after the interval when, just two balls into the over, Flintoff removed Lee, caught behind for 5.

Now 325-8, the mood was one of optimism as England strove to keep the lead down to sensible proportions. However, Warne continued to ride his luck and, with some powerful stroke play, pushed the scoring on quickly with Clark who was also taking full advantage of some inviting deliveries.

As Anderson, in particular, along with the other English seamers, struggled for any luck, both Warne and Clark raced the total forward. Warne, looking confident in his partner's ability, played with freedom to register his twelfth Test-match fifty as Clark moved into the thirties.

With the lead now stretched to an imposing 100 runs, the bowlers' heads began to drop but, eventually, an aerial stroke was to find a fielder as Clark miss-hit a pull stroke straight up into the air to fall for a comfortable catch to Pietersen at cover.

Now McGrath, in probably his last Test innings, came to join his fellow veteran in the middle as he attempted to reach his maiden Test hundred. Now aware that time in the middle was likely to be limited by his bowling partner's ability as a batsman, Warne attempted to hit out at every opportunity. This was soon to be his downfall and, with a tremendously entertaining 71 on the board, he came down the wicket to a Panesar delivery only to swing and miss, leaving Read the simplest of stumping opportunities.

Beginning 102 runs behind the Australians, the openers got off to the worst possible start as Strauss

PUSHING HIS LUCK: Warne, keen to entertain in his final innings, finally takes on too much as he comes down the wicket to a Monty delivery

NO LET-UP: Collingwood avoids another hostile delivery

Brisbane

Adelaide

Perth

Melbourne

Sydney

ducked into a Lee bouncer and took a nasty blow to the side of the helmet. Briefly, slumping down in his crease, he was quickly surrounded by a worried Lee and other concerned fielders. Thankfully, after a few minutes' recovery, he resumed his innings and appeared to be unaffected by the blow.

Soon after the incident Cook, caught in two minds to a short Lee delivery, top edged an attempted pull shot and sent the ball high in the air for an easy catch to Gilchrist, ending his series with a disappointing 4 runs.

Bell then came to the middle and, following on from the first innings, looked pretty comfortable at the crease and, with Strauss, the two of them steadily brought things under control as they went into tea on 43-1.

However, having added just a few more runs to his score, Strauss, perhaps still shaken, was beaten by

a decent Clark delivery that swung back into his pads and trapped him in front for 29.

With both openers back in the pavilion and still 52 runs from making Australia bat again, Pietersen came to the middle to join Bell in an attempt to build a target for the home team.

Restricted for runs by some excellent tight bowling from the Australians, both batsmen plugged away without a great deal of success and, as the drying up of runs increased the frustration and tension in the batsmen, it was Bell who was to crack first, slashing at a shortish ball outside his off stump and top edging it through to Gilchrist for a disappointing 28.

Now 59-3, the Aussies had Collingwood at the crease with the tourists still yet to pass into the black. Again bowling with great control and some superb fielding, England struggled to get any momentum to their innings but, with decent concentration and application, both players edged the total forward as the final session drew to a close.

Having made a typically gritty 17, Clark was to deceive Collingwood with a slow leg-cutter and, as Paul pushed out at the ball a little early, he succeeded only in offering a chance wide of Hayden in the gully which the big man did well to get across to.

England had now lost 4 wickets and were still 10 runs from taking their score into the positives as the captain came to the middle.

Warne, who had bowled only the one over in the innings so far, had been rested for the whole of the session to this point as, quite understandably, he was beginning to show a little weariness from his efforts. However, as is so often the case in his career, he could not be written off and, no sooner was he

back in the attack than the Australians were celebrating another wicket. Having scraped into a slender lead of just 6 runs, Warne drew Flintoff slightly out of his ground to push at a delivery that bit and turn pasted his outstretched defensive shot. Gilchrist, alert to the chance, quickly removed the bails and claimed the stumping with just millimetres to spare.

At 108-5, England were now in desperate trouble and, with only a few overs left until the close, Monty Panesar was promoted up the order to resist the rampant Australian attack.

With Pietersen, now in familiar territory of partnering the tail, he and Monty successfully saw off the remaining deliveries to leave themselves a huge task for the morning.

View from the Boundary

Sydney

Melbourne

Perth

Adelaide

Brisbane

PERFECT PARTNERS: Retirees Warne and McGrath exit the SCG together at the end of Australia's first innings

ASHES *frontline*

Thursday
04 January 2007

FIFTH TEST, DAY THREE

Things started just as we wanted as Mike Hussey went with only two runs added. Jimmy had him caught behind and we are thinking "here we go". Adam Gilchrist came in and went at it hard from the start as he had done in Perth. He squirted a couple through gully early on and then decided that if the ball was pitched up he was going to try and smack it out of the ground.

We were thinking that if we could take the last four wickets for 50 or 60 and end up no more than 20 or 30 behind on first innings we would have a cracking chance. But Shane Warne came out and changed all that. He swept Monty first ball and got an under-edge to send the ball past the wicket-keeper for four, at which point Paul Collingwood has decided to have a go at him from slip, which was not the best of ideas.

The last time we had a go at Warney was just before he took four wickets for not very many at Adelaide so we knew how he reacts to being wound up. He and Colly had a bit of a set-to – "My dad's bigger than your dad", that sort of thing – and umpire Billy Bowden had to come over and give them both a lollipop while the game was held up for five minutes.

When play resumed Warney got on with his job and hit the next ball for six. The confrontation definitely lifted him and put a spring in his step. Wrong man to wind up, Colly.

We were able to get rid of Gilchrist and Brett Lee before the lead got meaningful, but Stuart Clark came in with no pressure and rode his luck to score 35 vital runs in partnership with Warne.

I went from bowling 16 overs on the second day and being our best bowler to sending down seven overs in four spells today, something which led to an exchange of words between me and my great mate the skipper.

He had bowled six overs and I replaced him only for him to bring himself back after I had only sent down one over. Then after he had bowled one over I went back on, Clark hit me for four and squirted me over extra-cover for three, and I was taken off again. Toys were thrown at that point and let's say a friendly argument followed. Nothing sinister – just a few toys thrown at each other.

As it turned out, Saj Mahmood then came on and took a wicket in his first over so I had to run to Freddie and say: "Sorry mate, that's why you're captain and I'm not."

Australia ended up scoring 393 for a lead of 102, which although substantial was by no means necessarily a winning advantage.

We needed to bat well and chip away at it.

Despite losing Alastair Cook early on, we did seem to be getting into a reasonable position at 50-1 and then 93-3, but we kept losing wickets just when we seemed to be turning things around. Even so, with Kevin Pietersen and Andrew Flintoff together and the scores about level we still felt we could make a total that would put Australia under some pressure in their final innings.

The odd ball was starting to keep low and Monty would be in the game because the pitch was turning so 150 might have taken some getting.

Unfortunately for us, in the penultimate over of the day Fred lost his balance a bit trying to play as far forward as possible to Warne and just crept out of his crease as Adam Gilchrist removed the bails. He thought he had made it back in, but the TV replays proved different and it was a body blow for us. We closed on 114-5, only 12 runs in front.

THE PERFECT START: England delight at the early wicket of Hussey

Thursday
04 January 2007

FIFTH TEST, DAY THREE

The newspapers made for interesting reading this morning. Whether they are trying to conjure interest for the series, or whether they really believe England had us against the ropes is a matter for discussion, but it was as if England had us exactly where they wanted us.

From my eyes, the contest was pretty even going into this, day three, but the papers seemed to think we were gone. History shows you should never write off this Australian cricket team, even doubt our position, and by stumps tonight we once again proved what an incredible team we have.

Even though Michael Hussey went early we were still able to get

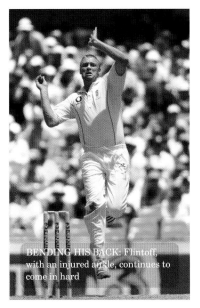

BENDING HIS BACK: Flintoff, with an injured ankle, continues to come in hard

ourselves 100 runs ahead of England. Shane Warne was the star with the bat, hitting the ball to all parts of the SCG while Adam Gilchrist and Andrew Symonds made fantastic contributions in tough batting conditions.

A controversial incident today was the dismissal of our vice-captain and wicket-keeper. Billy Bowden gave him out caught behind when it looked on the replay like he had missed the ball quite clearly. Known as a 'walker', I can only imagine Gilly's frustration when he returned to the changing room. He could be excused for wondering what the point of his walking is, if he still gets given out like he did today. The umpires generally know he walks when he is dismissed so you would have thought he would have had a few credits up his sleeve. Obviously today this wasn't the case.

In many ways it was incredible we were able to get 100 runs ahead but at the end of the day it has been our ability to win the big moments and conquer the big sessions that has had us in such a

position of strength this summer. Going into the second innings with such a lead changes the complex of the match, especially on a pitch like the SCG. It never gets easier to bat here, so every first-innings run is like gold.

Our lead again had England's batsmen under immense pressure from the start. This advantage was backed up by the way our bowlers teamed up this afternoon. Their pressure basically stole any of England's early-morning hopes of a final Test victory. Glenn McGrath was like a Rolls Royce as he bowled a line and length which made run scoring almost impossible. He was magnificent and is the main reason why we enter tomorrow as unbackable favourites to win this Test and whitewash this series. In his final Test he demonstrated why he has arguably been Australia's finest fast bowler.

BITING HIS LIP: Gilchrist, having not walked, gets a poor decision on 62

View from the Boundary

Friday
05 January 2007

FIFTH TEST, DAY FOUR

England began the day just 12 runs ahead of the home side as they attempted to build as large a lead as possible for the Australians to chase.

Just 2 balls into the day though, and with no addition to the lead, McGrath got Pietersen to push at one outside his off stump to give Glen, in his last Test match, the prized wicket of England's leading batsman as Kevin edged a simple catch through to Gilchrist for 29.

With six down, Read came to the middle and, keen to get off the mark as soon as possible, set off for a sharp single in the first over he faced. Monty, backing up, did his best to make the ground but, with the lightning-fast Symonds moving quickly onto the ball, his fate was sealed as, with a tremendous direct hit, Panesar was left a foot short of his ground for 0.

Now 114-7 Read was joined by Mahmood and, facing an Australian attack that was determined to get the job done as quickly as possible, Read flirted nervously with a shortish Lee delivery and edged the ball for an excellent diving catch from Ponting in the slips for just 4.

At 122-8 England's fate was almost sealed as Harmison came to join his fast-bowling buddy and it was not long later when McGrath, bowling a useful off-cutter that kept a little low to Mahmood, had the batsman nowhere near it and, still just 21 runs ahead of Australia, the ninth wicket went down as the ball clattered into his stumps.

Harmison now, in a show of last-minute defiance, swung and collected a few deliveries from Warne and McGrath to push the lead up past 40. However, soon enough, Glen was to fittingly finish things off as, with a well-delivered slower ball, he had Anderson sky an easy catch to Hussey at mid-on to finish the innings a mere 45 runs ahead.

With just 46 required to complete a series whitewash, Langer,

THE LAST BATTLE: KP strides onto the field of play to resume his innings

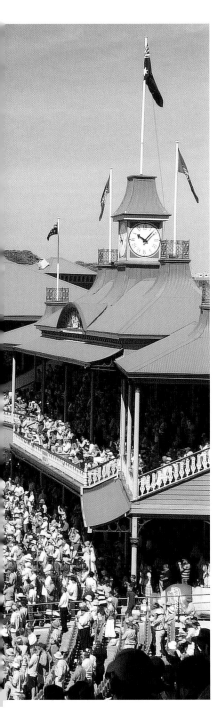

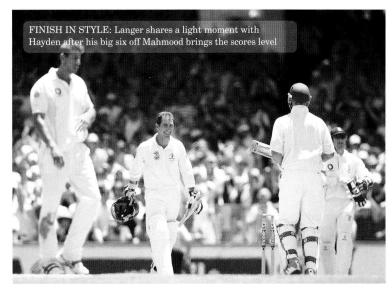

FINISH IN STYLE: Langer shares a light moment with Hayden after his big six off Mahmood brings the scores level

loss, they played with understandable confidence as they quickly began to eat away at England's slender lead.

Finally, in just the eleventh over of the innings, Australia, with a huge six and a single, finished off their fifth consecutive win of the series with a huge 10-wicket victory and completed a remarkable Ashes contest whitewash for the first time since the 1920s.

THE END OF A GREAT CAREER: McGrath bids his farewells to Test-match cricket

through a guard of honour, came to the crease for the last time with his good friend Matthew Hayden. Both keen to see the task off without

Brisbane

Adelaide

Perth

Melbourne

Sydney

View from the Boundary

MARK OF RESPECT: the England team form a guard of honour for Langer

ASHES *frontline*

Brisbane

Adelaide

Perth

Melbourne

Sydney

Friday

05 January 2007

FIFTH TEST, DAY FOUR

While Kevin Pietersen is at the crease anything is possible. So when the day started with KP unbeaten on 29 there was still hope for us but, this time, Kev was out before a run was added, edging McGrath to Gilchrist in the first over.

Once that happened reality hit home and we knew the writing was firmly on the wall. Monty was run out and again we subsided pretty quickly, although I was able to enjoy a last-wicket stand of 24 with Jimmy Anderson to delay more Aussie celebrations.

I've actually batted for quite a long time in the series, but almost always in situations where I had to dig in and try to support the batsman at the other end.

When Stuart Clark went in at ten for Australia he had the freedom to play his shots because of the score

ONE LAST TIME: Flintoff leads his men out for the final innings of the series

LAST HOPE: KP heads back to the pavilion having added no more runs to his overnight total

already on the board. I can't help feeling a bit envious, but I enjoyed the challenge of facing Warne and McGrath and was reasonably happy with how I competed against them.

Australia were left with just 46 to win and it was a great moment for Justin Langer when he came out to open their innings with Matthew Hayden for the last time.

I was given the new ball and managed to make Langer hop about a bit, not having bowled to him that much since that infamous opening delivery in Brisbane.

Walking off at the end of the game I told Justin Langer that I hadn't seen much of him for six weeks and didn't want to let him go out without a few rib-ticklers.

He certainly rates as one of the toughest opening batsmen I've ever played against. You can hit him as many times as you like and he's still in there fighting, which can be very deflating for a fast bowler.

Justin's had a great career and perhaps we'll meet up again one day in English county cricket now that

he has agreed to captain Somerset in 2007. He will be a terrific influence there, that's for sure.

Obviously, it was a difficult time for the England players when the game ended. We went over to thank the Barmy Army for their fantastic support and then had to watch the Australians celebrating in the same mad way we had done at the end of the 2005 series. You have to put on a brave face when in front of the public, but back in the dressing room our sense of disappointment was huge and it didn't get any better for the next four days as far as I was concerned. My family were with me, but I was right out of it, so desperate did it feel to have lost 5-0. This game of ours offers great highs when you win and that's what we are all in it for, but when you lose it is bloody tough. Watching our celebrations in 2005 strengthened the Australian players' resolve not to have to do it again and I'm sure the same will apply with England as we try to put this tour behind us and look to the future.

Sydney · Melbourne · Perth · Adelaide · Brisbane

Friday

05 January 2007

FIFTH TEST, DAY FOUR

Today felt like a fairytale. Glenn McGrath took the last wicket, I was there at the end with my long-time opening partner Matty Hayden, and we walked off knowing we had just beaten England five-nil. It was quite a surreal feeling when Matt hit the winning runs and the aftermath of such an achievement was unbelievable.

From the moment Kevin Pietersen was out in the first over, until the moment I went to bed last night, it was as if I were in a dream.

England's tail again crumbled to the suffocating pressure of our bowlers and our fielding was as sharp as I have ever seen it. Right until the end we showed just how much this series has meant to us.

I was overawed by England's gesture of forming a guard of honour for me to walk through. There can be no greater sign of respect than what England showed me today and for that I am eternally grateful. As I walked through I smiled at Freddie Flintoff and asked him if he would mind bowling me a few half volleys to help me through my last Test innings. With that he just smiled and told me the guard of honour was the only luxury I should expect for the rest of the day.

He meant what he said because Steve Harmison bowled like the wind for an hour; cracking my rib and bruising my hand in the process. It was as if my last memory of Test cricket should be one of the tough and torrid times I have endured as an opening batsman. My big mate from Durham didn't let me down as he bowled as fast and

aggressive as he had all series. In many ways Harmy is a bit of an enigma, but when he finds his rhythm he is without doubt one of the most uncomfortable bowlers in the world to face.

With seven runs to get I winked at Matty and said 'a six and a one would be the perfect ending buddy.' I was feeling a bit emotional at the occasion and as if to equal England's sign of respect he smiled and then hit Sajid Mahmood for a massive six, before caressing the winning run through the covers.

A couple of seconds after the job was completed I stood and embraced my opening partner and best mate, and choked back the tears. Right at that moment it struck me I would never bat with him again and for this I felt sad. Fortunately, the enormity of the moment meant my sadness was quickly replaced by jubilation and for the next three quarters of an hour we sucked in the triumphant atmosphere.

Straight after the win our changing room was filled with

family, friends and supporters, including our Prime Minister, John Howard. The England team also came into the rooms and stayed until about 7pm. Despite their humiliating loss it was great to have a final beer with the England boys. I am sure, if they use this disappointment to their advantage, they will be a stronger team for the experience.

On returning to the team hotel we then were invited onto the boat of James Packer where we sang the team song at about midnight and reflected on what has been five of the best weeks of our lives.

It has been suggested that England were poor this summer but in my view we were so committed to this series that even with every one of their injured players available we would have won this series. It was our goal at the start of the series to make the gap between us and England as big as possible, and as I sit here typing I know this ambition has been achieved.

THE ULTIMATE PRIZE: Langer lifts the Ashes trophy in recognition of the crowd's support

View from the Boundary

THE PERFECT RESULT FROM THE WORLD'S BEST TEAM: The Australians pose for a photograph to mark their historic 5-0 series victory

Brisbane

Adelaide

Perth

Melbourne

Sydney

Scorecard

England 1st Innings

			Runs	Balls	4s	6s
A J Strauss	c A C Gilchrist	b B Lee	29	52	3	0
A N Cook	c A C Gilchrist	b S R Clark	20	47	2	0
I R Bell		b G D McGrath	71	153	8	0
K P Pietersen	c M E K Hussey	b G D McGrath	41	104	1	0
P D Collingwood	c A C Gilchrist	b G D McGrath	27	73	4	0
A Flintoff	c A C Gilchrist	b S R Clark	89	142	11	1
C M W Read	c A C Gilchrist	b B Lee	2	9	0	0
S I Mahmood	c M L Hayden	b B Lee	0	1	0	0
S J Harmison	lbw	b S R Clark	2	24	0	0
M S Panesar	lbw	b S K Warne	0	14	0	0
J M Anderson	not out		0	5	0	0
Extras		2nb 3w 5lb	10			
Total		all out	291	(103.4 ovs)		

Bowling	O	M	R	W
G D McGrath	29	8	67	3
B Lee	22	5	75	3
S R Clark	24	6	62	3
S K Warne	22.4	1	69	1
A Symonds	6	2	13	0

Fall of wicket

45 (A J Strauss), 58 (A N Cook), 166 (K P Pietersen), 167 (I R Bell), 245 (P D Collingwood), 258 (C M W Read), 258 (S I Mahmood), 282 (S J Harmison), 291 (A Flintoff), 291 (M S Panesar)

Australia 1st Innings

			Runs	Balls	4s	6s
J L Langer	c C M W Read	b J M Anderson	26	27	4	0
M L Hayden	c P D Collingwood	b S J Harmison	33	77	5	0
R T Ponting	run out		45	72	6	0
M E K Hussey	c C M W Read	b J M Anderson	37	100	3	1
M J Clarke	c C M W Read	b S J Harmison	11	24	1	0
A Symonds		b M S Panesar	48	95	6	0
A C Gilchrist	c C M W Read	b J M Anderson	62	71	8	0
S K Warne	st C M W Read	b M S Panesar	71	65	9	2
B Lee	c C M W Read	b A Flintoff	5	10	1	0
S R Clark	c K P Pietersen	b S I Mahmood	35	41	1	0
G D McGrath	not out		0	3	0	0
Extras		6nb 4w 10lb	20			
Total		all out	393	(96.3 ovs)		

Bowling	O	M	R	W
A Flintoff	17	2	56	1
J M Anderson	26	8	98	3
S J Harmison	23	5	80	2
S I Mahmood	11	1	59	1
M S Panesar	19.3	0	90	2

Fall of wicket

34 (J L Langer), 100 (M L Hayden), 118 (R T Ponting), 155 (M J Clarke), 190 (M E K Hussey), 260 (A Symonds), 318 (A C Gilchrist), 325 (B Lee), 393 (S R Clark), 393 (S K Warne)

ASHES *frontline*

England 2nd Innings

			Runs	Balls	4s	6s
A J Strauss	lbw	b S R Clark	24	45	3	0
A N Cook	c A C Gilchrist	b B Lee	4	8	1	0
I R Bell	c A C Gilchrist	b B Lee	28	51	5	0
K P Pietersen	c A C Gilchrist	b G D McGrath	29	95	3	0
P D Collingwood	c M L Hayden	b S R Clark	17	36	3	0
A Flintoff	st A C Gilchrist	b S K Warne	7	21	1	0
M S Panesar	run out		0	19	0	0
C M W Read	c R T Ponting	b B Lee	4	17	1	0
S I Mahmood		b G D McGrath	4	11	1	0
S J Harmison	c M E K Hussey		16	26	2	0
J M Anderson		b G D McGrath	5	22	0	0
Extras		3nb 1w 2b 3lb	9			
Total		all out	**147**	(58.0 ovs)		

Bowling	O	M	R	W
B Lee	14	5	39	3
G D McGrath	21	11	38	3
S R Clark	12	4	29	2
S K Warne	6	1	23	1
A Symonds	5	2	13	0

Fall of wicket

5 (A N Cook), 55 (A J Strauss), 64 (I R Bell), 98 (P D Collingwood), 113 (A Flintoff), 114 (K P Pietersen), 114 (M S Panesar), 122 (C M W Read), 123 (S I Mahmood), 147 (J M Anderson)

Australia 2nd Innings

			Runs	Balls	4s	6s
J L Langer	not out		20	43	2	0
M L Hayden	not out		23	22	2	1
Extras		3lb	20			
Total		for 0	**46**	(10.5 ovs)		

Bowling	O	M	R	W
J M Anderson	4	0	12	0
S J Harmison	5	1	13	0
S I Mahmood	1.5	0	18	0

Fall of wicket

Australia beat England by 10 wickets

Post-Series
Epilogue

Sydney

Melbourne

Perth

Adelaide

Brisbane

Steve Harmison

Tuesday

16 January 2007

What went wrong? In terms of preparation I don't think the team could have done much more in the circumstances, but I personally could have been better prepared. With hindsight, because I didn't play in the South Australia game at Adelaide I didn't get sufficient overs under my belt before the First Test. But as I explained I did have a little niggle in my side at the time and if I had played against South Australia and broken down everyone would have thought how stupid it was. A decision was taken not to risk me with the First Test just around the corner. It was the right decision, but it meant I did go into the Brisbane Test under-prepared. I still felt in good enough form, but that first ball to second slip shot my confidence to pieces and it took some time to get it back.

People say we might have gone to Australia a week earlier and arranged one more game in the build-up to the First Test, but I don't think that was really possible.

What I do believe is that the ICC Trophy was exceptionally badly timed as far as the England team were concerned.

We had come off the back of a hard domestic season and had it not taken place we could have had a decent break before taking on something as big as an Ashes tour.

I know people will say Australia won the ICC Trophy, but they had had a five-month break before that and talking to their players during the series I know how much they appreciated that.

We had a tough winter followed by a demanding summer followed

by an ICC Trophy followed by the Ashes followed by the World Cup. You are talking about 14 months of virtual non-stop cricket. We have to look at the amount of cricket we are playing and the amount of travelling involved if we want to keep our top players performing to the peak of their ability when it matters most. We were hungry and desperate to win the Ashes series, but we were not as fresh as we could have been.

There has been criticism of the selection of Marcus Trescothick and Ashley Giles for the tour because of the uncertainty that existed about Marcus's health and the fact that Ash had been out of cricket for so long through injury. But I maintain that the squad selected was right and the best available. Both Marcus and Ash have been huge players for us.

In hindsight, which is always a wonderful thing, Andrew Flintoff did have an awful lot on his plate as England captain and our top all-rounder. But at the time of his appointment he was the right man to be skipper. He was the best man for the job, simple as that. Now the tour is over it's easy to say that perhaps too much was asked of him. But he handled himself superbly throughout a tour which might have seen a lesser person crack. He took each setback on the chin and in some ways even enhanced his reputation. I'm proud to call him a mate and I honestly don't believe our fortunes would have been any different under another captain.

One criticism that really irked me was that we struggled because, having been awarded MBEs for our success in 2005 and doing the open-top bus trip to Trafalgar Square, we somehow felt we had achieved all there was to achieve.

What upset me most is that Paul Collingwood has been singled out

ASHES *frontline*

THROUGH THICK AND THIN: The England players applaud the endless support of the English fans through what had been a difficult series for all

Brisbane

Adelaide

Perth

Melbourne

Sydney

Post-Series Epilogue

Sydney

Melbourne

Perth

Adelaide

Brisbane

by a lot of people as not having deserved his MBE because he didn't contribute as much as some other players to our victory. Colly didn't write to the Queen to say "give me an MBE". Nor for that matter did Michael Vaughan write to Ken Livingstone and ask if the England team could go on an open-top bus tour through London. Are people saying Colly should have turned down an MBE? How many of them would do that?

As for Trafalgar Square, the bus journey made us all look like lager louts because we'd been out celebrating gaining the Ashes the night before, I can't believe many people would not have done the same. The players would have preferred the public celebrations a couple of days after the last day at the Oval, but we were told when to appear. I wonder how the rugby lads would have looked on a bus the day after their World Cup success. Those scenes where we all looked the worse for wear have now come back to haunt us. Maybe they were over the top, but they provided some great memories for us and many other people and they were not of our own making.

I was criticised personally for the way I responded to a question in an interview carried out during the Fifth Test. I was asked what I would be doing when I got back home and I said I'd have to ask the coach. Even Duncan Fletcher asked me about this because I think he and those listening to the interview were expecting me to say I was going back to play for Durham and work as hard as possible in preparation for this summer's Test matches.

I have to defend myself because my response was a result of what had happened to me last year when I got asked about my plans following an injury and I told everyone I would be playing for

PRACTICE MAKES PERFECT: Harmison continues to get overs 'under his belt' at the MCG. His continued improvement through the series perhaps highlighted his lack of preparation

ASHES *frontline*

TIME FOR REFLECTION: The tough times in Australia will "drive me on" for more success in the future

Durham against Warwickshire in a county match.

I was getting on the bus to go to that game when I got a phone call saying I wasn't allowed to play by the ECB. It was felt I had bowled enough against Yorkshire and they stopped me from playing. Having told everyone in the press, that I would be involved against Warwickshire I got criticised when it didn't happen and had to explain that the ECB pay my wages and therefore decide when I should and shouldn't play.

When things didn't go very well for me in the following one-day series for England I got more criticism for not playing against Warwickshire and being under-prepared. So when this time I was asked by Michael Atherton when my next game would be and what I would be doing when I got home I could have talked about Durham's pre-season games and the opening County Championship fixtures, but didn't want to be left with egg on my face again.

The bottom line is that we were up against one of the best sides ever to have played the game. We went into the series confident, but my personal view deep down was that we would have to play out of our skins and four or five of us might even have to perform beyond our maximum to come out on top.

Instead, only two or three of us played to our maximum and the rest, myself included, failed to find our best form.

Australia on the other hand had players like Michael Clarke, Mike Hussey and Stuart Clark who did play beyond even their own expectations. And even Ricky Ponting, in my opinion the best batsman in the world, wouldn't have dreamed of having the sort of series he did before it started. Then just when we were down along came Andrew Symonds, who to start with looked like getting out every time we bowled to him, to score 150. You can look for all the excuses in the world but the top and bottom of it is that we were beaten fair and square by a better side.

Losing 5-0 was a gut-wrenching experience. The way I felt on the flight home and the four days which preceded it I wouldn't wish on anyone. It was a sick feeling and one of the worst experiences I've ever had. But it will drive me on, just as it did to the Australian players when they experienced it in 2005. The next Ashes battle will not feature Messrs Warne, McGrath and Langer, who have been such magnificent servants to Australia. We need to start planning now how we are going to win it. I know I want to be involved.

Brisbane

Adelaide

Perth

Melbourne

Sydney

Justin Langer

Tuesday
16 January 2007

A week after the end of the most fulfilling series of my career, I am still pinching myself at what has been. In many ways I can't believe it is all over. For sixteen months I dreamed about winning back the Ashes. There has hardly been a moment when the thought of retaining the little urn hasn't crossed my mind.

Losing them in England hurt; in fact it more than hurt, it really hurt and we steeled ourselves to get them back no matter what. Before the series began we took three important themes into the contest. Firstly, we wanted to avoid all distractions that would detract from our performance. Secondly, we vowed to back ourselves to 'make the shot' every time and finally we decided the tough periods were only as tough as we wanted to make them. In other words we needed to stay focused and committed to the cause, play with positive intent and absorb every pressure situation that came our way.

By achieving these goals we knew we would accomplish our ultimate mission which was to demonstrate without doubt that we are the best team in the world and that the gap between Australia and England was a wide one. Admittedly we played hard ball in order to win back the Ashes and we weren't as 'matey' as we were the last time we met England, but as I sit here right now, I feel like every minute of planning and hard work has been worth the effort.

There is an old saying that 'the pain of discipline is nothing like the pain of disappointment' and I can say without hesitation that the cornerstone behind our success in this series has been discipline. We executed our skills well, we won the big moments and we made life uncomfortable for England by keeping them under constant pressure in every aspect of the game.

Throughout, our bowling group were magnificent. Led by Shane Warne, the greatest of all time, Glenn McGrath, Stuart Clark and Brett Lee made batting a miserable experience for England's batsmen. Besides Kevin Pietersen, and early on in the series Paul Collingwood, England's batsmen were almost suffocated out of the contest. All of them made a score at one stage or another but as a group they were outclassed and clinically decimated through sheer pressure by our bowling core.

Before the series we made a concerted and planned effort to work tirelessly on our catching and besides a few mishaps, our ability to snap up most chances played a significant role in the final outcome. Having the likes of Andrew Symonds, Michael Clarke and Michael Hussey in the ring, just adds to the pressure on any batting team and it makes the hours spent fielding an exciting adventure when these guys are your team-mates.

In the batting department, every one of our batsmen made a contribution. As always our captain

END OF AN ERA: McGrath, Warne and Langer greet the cricket media for the last time together

was the leader of the pack. He was so determined leading into this series and his mountain of runs just acted as proof of this. The greatest strength of any cricket captain is their ability to lead by example and here we saw the world's number one batsman dominate the opponent while proving his tactical nous over and over again. In my view this series marks Ricky as a 'great' captain.

I said after the first day's play that I had to wonder if the first ball by Steve Harmison would prove to be significant. Had he bowled his now famous delivery to second slip in the second over of the game or even on the second ball of the game, no one would have blinked an eye at it, but the fact was he didn't. The first ball of the most

hyped-up series of our lives was a wide one which thudded into the waiting hands of his skipper at second slip. Thankfully it wasn't off the edge of my bat, but rather straight from Harmy's hand.

Out in the middle I still remember the reaction of his team-mates. Everything was silent, as if a balloon had been burst to mess up the party. I was out there looking for a fight to burn off some of my nerves and yet England's body language seemed flat and even a little intimidated. Obviously England will never admit this but I felt from the very first

hour that this England team was a lot different to the one that beat us only sixteen months before.

While we were still playing against a number of the same players the body language just looked and felt different, and in my view it was this key component which made the difference throughout.

Winning a series of this magnitude five-nil is a little hard to comprehend and while the result looks comprehensive it is never as easy as it may look. England had their chances, just as we had ours, but at the end of the day it was our

THE PERFECT ENDING: Langer and Ponting savour the atmosphere at the SCG at the end of the series

Brisbane

Adelaide

Perth

Melbourne

Sydney

Post-Series Epilogue

capacity to take the opportunities that led to the whitewash.

From your seat you may have wondered about the emotion displayed from the Australian team, especially in Adelaide, Perth and Sydney. I am certain the reason for this was because of our desire to regain the Ashes. In the sixteen months between battles we have played great Test cricket, having won all but one of our Tests, and we have planned and prepared vigorously for our revenge. We spent five days at a boot camp where we were deprived food, sleep and personal space, all in the quest for toughening our resolve for these last five weeks.

During that time in the bush we learned more about conquering our fears, performing as a team and eliminating distractions from the task at hand. Over the last few weeks we have put those lessons to work and as a result have enjoyed the fruits of our labours.

I know I will never play Test cricket again, but after this series I have to wonder if the game could ever get better than this. Not only was my retirement a perfectly scripted fairytale, but leaving the game with two great champions after a five-nil whitewash of our oldest rival is pretty much as good as it gets. After the last series I kept quoting a famous saying which states, 'the best thing in the world is to play and win, the second best thing in the world is to play and lose, as long as you are still playing.'

I loved the series in England for the sheer tension and pressure of the contest, but I have to say I have loved this series even more because not only was I still playing but this time we came out as the victors, and I will confess it is a much better feeling than how we were back on 12 September 2005.

WHITEWASH: The Australian team cover themselves in champagne as they begin their long and well-deserved celebrations

Post-Series Epilogue

Series Averages

England

Batting

Player	Matches	Inns	N/O	Runs	High Score	Average	100	50	Catches	Stump
K P Pietersen	5	10	1	490	158	54.44	1	3	3	0
P D Collingwood	5	10	1	433	206	48.11	1	1	7	0
I R Bell	5	10	0	331	87	33.1	0	4	5	0
A Flintoff	5	10	1	254	89	28.22	0	2	0	0
A N Cook	5	10	0	276	116	27.6	1	0	2	0
A J Strauss	5	10	0	247	50	24.7	0	1	3	0
A F Giles	2	4	1	74	27	24.66	0	0	1	0
C M W Read	2	4	1	35	26	11.66	0	0	11	1
G O Jones	3	6	0	63	33	10.5	0	0	9	0
S J Harmison	5	9	1	73	23	9.12	0	0	1	0
M S Panesar	3	6	1	35	16	7	0	0	0	0
J M Anderson	3	5	3	12	5	6	0	0	0	0
M J Hoggard	4	7	1	30	9	5	0	0	0	0
S I Mahmood	3	6	0	18	10	3	0	0	0	0

Bowling

Player	Overs	Maidens	Runs	Wkts	Average	Best	5w	10w
M J Hoggard3	141	25	486	13	37.38	7-109	1	0
M S Panesar	89.3	8	379	10	37.9	5-92	1	0
A Flintoff	137	18	481	11	43.72	4-99	0	0
S I Mahmood	51.2	4	264	5	52.8	4-100	0	0
S J Harmison	170.1	29	614	10	61.4	4-48	0	0
J M Anderson	93.2	18	413	5	82.6	3-98	0	0
A F Giles	82	9	262	3	87.33	1-46	0	0
I R Bell	1	0	12	0	0	0-0	0	0
P D Collingwood	3	0	20	0	0	0-0	0	0
K P Pietersen	29	2	125	0	0	0-0	0	0

Australia

Batting

Player	Matches	Inns	N/O	Runs	High Score	Average	100	50	Catches	Stump
M E K Hussey	5	7	2	458	103	91.6	1	4	5	0
R T Ponting	5	8	1	576	196	82.28	2	2	4	0
M J Clarke	5	7	2	389	135	77.8	2	1	2	0
A Symonds	3	4	0	232	156	58	1	0	3	0
M L Hayden	5	9	1	413	153	51.62	1	1	7	0
S K Warne	5	5	1	196	71	49	0	1	5	0
A C Gilchrist	5	6	1	229	102	45.8	1	2	24	2
J L Langer	5	9	2	303	100	43.28	1	1	5	0
B Lee	5	5	2	65	43	21.66	0	0	2	0
S R Clark	5	5	0	85	39	17	0	0	0	0
D R Martyn	2	3	0	45	29	15	0	0	3	0
G D McGrath	5	5	2	10	8	3.33	0	0	1	0

Bowling

Player	Overs	Maidens	Runs	Wkts	Average	Best	5w	10w
S R Clark	194.2	53	443	26	17.03	4-72	0	0
G D McGrath	209.1	65	502	21	23.9	6-50	1	0
S K Warne	241.2	43	698	23	30.34	5-39	1	0
B Lee	196.5	32	664	20	33.2	4-47	0	0
A Symonds	31	8	79	2	39.5	2-8	0	0
M E K Hussey	1	0	5	0	0	0-0	0	0
M J Clarke	17	2	53	0	0	0-0	0	0